Tokyo, the 'Eastern Capital', has only enjoyed that
name and status for 150 years. Before then, it was
Edo, a sprawling town by the bay; earlier still, it was
Edojuku, a medieval outpost overlooking farmlands;
and, thousands of years ago, its mudflats and marshes
were home to elephants, deer and marine life.

Jonathan Clements traces the city's fascinating
history from the first forest clearances and the
samurai wars to the hedonistic 'floating world' era
– and onward to the twentieth century with its
destruction and redevelopment, boom and bust.
With the 2020 Olympic Games on the horizon,
this is the story of how Tokyo became Japan's true
capital and an icon of vivid urban culture.

JONATHAN CLEMENTS is the author of many books about Japan, including *A Brief History of the Samurai*, *Anime: A History*, biographies of Admiral Tōgō and Prince Saionji, and *The Dorama Encyclopedia: A Guide to Japanese TV Drama Since 1953* (with Tamamuro Motoko). He wrote the 'Asia and the World' chapters for the Oxford University Press Big Idea history series for schools, which won an Australian Publishing Association award for Excellence in Educational Publishing in 2012. His recent books include *Christ's Samurai: The True Story of the Shimabara Rebellion* and *Modern Japan: All That Matters*. Since 2016, he has presented *Route Awakening*, a National Geographic TV series about icons of Chinese history and culture.

An Armchair Traveller's History of Tokyo

Jonathan Clements

Published in Great Britain in 2018 by
The Armchair Traveller at the bookHaus
4 Cinnamon Row, London SW11 3TW

A CIP catalogue record of this book is available from the British
Library

ISBN: 978-1-909961-58-6
eISBN: 978-1-909961-59-3

Typeset in Garamond by MacGuru Ltd

Printed and bound in the Czech Republic by Akcentmedia

For Motoko

Contents

Introduction

'EVERY VIEW was like a picture on a fan,' wrote Isabel Anderson of her trip through the Tokyo streets for an audience with the Taishō Emperor.

> We went on past the walled residence of ancient feudal lords; past the *torii* – the 'bird-rest' gates at temple entrances – through which we caught glimpses of stone lanterns and the wide-open fronts of picturesque shrines. Again, we passed tea-houses from which the twang of *samisen* was heard; and left behind us rows on rows of shops with wares of every kind exposed in front for trade. Everywhere the men and quaint little women went stumbling along on their clicking clogs, bowing low to one another; and every moment through some opening of wall or entrance we could see delightful little gardens of tree and stone and water arranged in a way both fascinating and fanciful.

The year was 1912. Much of Tokyo was a ramshackle slum of low wooden buildings. Parts lay derelict, deserted by the last of the samurai a generation earlier and left to fall into ruin. Others were shanty towns of vagrants, or workshops belching industrial smog, the streets drowned beneath the din of clanking trams and noisy factories. Anderson, the wife of the newly appointed US ambassador, chose to see a fairy-tale Japan straight out of *The Mikado*, and in doing so managed to encapsulate much of the country's orientalist appeal to its foreign visitors.

'Many Japanese will tell you,' wrote the humourist George Mikes in 1970, 'that Tokyo is an ugly city. You must not disagree with them because that would be discourteous; you must not agree with them either, because that would be even more discourteous. You say: "Beauty is in the eye of the beholder."' Mourning much of the urban renewal that had accompanied the 1964 Olympics, Mikes thought the place had already gone to the dogs – not that he gave it much of a chance to begin with. 'London is a galaxy of countless villages,' he wrote, 'but Tokyo is an overgrown small town... a dreary conglomeration of houses without a real centre'.

Tokyo, the 'Eastern Capital', has only enjoyed that name and status for the last 150 years. Before then it was Edo (meaning 'Estuary'), a sprawling town by the bay, which was briefly the largest city in the world. Before then, it was the site of Edojuku (meaning 'Estuary Lodge'), a medieval outpost that kept watch over farming estates. Whereas the imperial court ruled Japan from the sleepy city of Kyōto in the south, the landowners of the plains beyond the mountains held the true wealth and power, which they eventually asserted in a series of civil wars.

In the seventeenth century, the region became the administrative centre of Japan's Shōgun overlords and the site of a vibrant, vivid urban culture of theatres, taverns and brothels. After the Meiji Restoration in 1868, it became the true capital, home to the Emperors, seat of government and site of rapid urban growth. Today, Tokyo is home to some 13 million people – or, if one wants to include the suburbs, 37.8 million. To put it another way, this book about a single 'city' is obliged to address a contemporary population larger than that of Peru. Nor is it merely a cluster of districts around Tokyo Bay; modern Tokyo's reach and infrastructure extends deep into nearby Yokohama, Chiba and Saitama, and, thanks to a quirk of political administration, more than 1,000 kilometres to the south along the Ogasawara island chain, all the way to Iwo Jima.

It can be difficult to separate what is required of a history of Tokyo from a history of Japan in general. Tokyo has been a nexus of power and people for a thousand years, which has made it crucial to historical events in the whole country. Throughout the period of the Tokugawa Shōgunate (1600–1868), for example, the enforced attendance of feudal lords in Edo ensured that the city was a crossroads in customs and styles. Whatever the cool kids were doing in the Shōgun's city soon made it out into the provinces; whatever new fad had caught on in the provinces was sure to be picked up in Edo by the time that season's samurai had rotated back to their home towns. By the twentieth century such cultural dominance was fixed even more firmly, as radio and then television broadcasts ensured that the capital's argot and slang, its gossip and its fads, were swiftly transmitted to the periphery.

This can even influence historiography – the story of history itself – since Tokyo is usually the place where visitors are most likely to make landfall. It is Tokyo, for example, where Edward S. Morse first began documenting the archaeology of ancient Japan – but he found it *there* because he was taking up a post at the Imperial University (now named the University of Tokyo). Later researchers have determined that the earliest extant examples of Jōmon pottery are to be found far to the south, but the original 'discovery' was a Tokyo event.

Although all cities see land usages come and go, Tokyo is more susceptible than most to sudden transformations in its appearance. Out in the suburbs, its districts derive their names from farms and roadhouses assimilated by the growing samurai-era sprawl. In 1878, the traveller Isabella Bird wrote in some disappointment to her sister that although she had boarded a train to 'Tokyo', she was forced to get off at either Shinagawa or Shinbashi, 'two of the many villages that have grown together into the capital'. Tokyo, for her, was difficult to point to, a catch-all title for a cluster of districts without a real centre or identity.

The outlines of many of Tokyo's wards were defined by sudden crises – fires, floods or quakes that left pockets of land ripe for renewal. Sometimes these crises have been political: the overnight departure of the samurai lords, leaving their mansion quarter derelict, or the end of the US Occupation, leaving multiple military bases ready for redevelopment. But few of these events have been met with the necessary remedial funding or long-term oversight. After the great earthquake of 1923, Mayor Gotō Shinpei hoped to create a new ultra-modern city, but was forced to cut back until only one of his planned thoroughfares survived. The tangle of small landholdings often makes it difficult to requisition a large enough space for something truly different and wide ranging – only 5% of Tokyo's space is devoted to parkland, compared to 30% in London.

Many of Tokyo's place names allude to now-levelled hills, lost river valleys, demolished gates and watchtowers or long-since-relocated temples. Centuries of land rec-lamation have created entirely new districts, walling off former dockyards and clifftops from the sea. Place names commemorate bridges over canals that no longer exist, 'islands' that are now a mile from the sea and natural features that are little more than folk memories. **Akasaka**, meaning 'Red Slope', was once a riot of crimson-rooted madder plants. **Kamata**, the 'Plum Fields', was once a wide set of orchards. **Nerima**, the 'Tethered Horses', was the place where samurai cavalrymen once trained their steeds. When the horses were gone, the land was given over to market gardens, and subsequently lent its name to a particular kind of giant radish. When the railways came, the land was prized more for residence and industry, and now only the name remains.

The early modern city was largely constructed from wood, making it relatively easy for certain landmarks to physically move from their original sites. Many historic buildings began in other locations, but have been packed up and relocated at least once – such as the cluster of temples that fled the digging of the Edo Castle moat to be rebuilt in Yotsuya. Close-packed lumber and paper walls also made the city vulnerable to fires, leading to several conflagrations in its history that wiped entire districts off the map. The Kantō Earthquake of 1923 and the worst of the air raids of 1945 are only the most recent in a procession of disasters that have altered the city throughout its history, destroying great swathes of its past. Many are the occasions when we Tokyo wanderers find ourselves in a park that was once a slum, a peaceful temple precinct that was once a swamp or an entire district named after a feature that either no longer exists, or never happened. Most notoriously **Kabukichō** ('Kabuki Town') derives its name from a post-war plan to revitalise a ruined area with a kabuki theatre, which never quite made it off the drawing board. Instead, the neighbourhood became a magnet for immigrants and the underclass, and evolved into a centre of organised crime and prostitution – a seedy maze of bars and massage parlours, still retaining the name concocted by its planners. Today, it clings to and rather enjoys this edgy reputation, despite the departure of many of its underworld associations over the last decade.

I have translated many of the meanings of Tokyo place names in an effort to demystify allusions to forgotten events and land uses that are obvious to Japanese speakers. Thus, **Saitama** is 'the Land over the Tama River', **Gunma** is the place of the 'Horse Herds', **Toshigi** is the place of the 'Horse Chestnut Trees' and **Ibaraki** is the site of the hastily constructed eighth-century stronghold 'Thornbush Fort'. Sometimes, place names simply derive from forgotten landowners (such as **Chiba**, the 'Thousand Leaves'), or even the transcription of old words with a forgotten meaning, such as the Tama River, the name of which has multiple possible origins, none of them confirmed. But where such a provenance is still manifest, I include it in my text. An appreciation of Tokyo's history is greatly aided by knowing that **Ginza** was the 'Silver Mint' and **Odaiba** was the 'Gun Batteries'. These meanings are often immediately apparent to Tokyo locals and, I believe, help bring the city's historical development to light, even on a contemporary subway trip.

Even old George Mikes changed his mind eventually, conceding that Tokyo wasn't all bad. 'Tokyo may lack architectural beauty,' he confessed, 'but it has a character and excitement; it is alive. I found it a mysterious and lovable city.'

1

The Kantō Plain: Prehistory to the 1200s

IN THE BEGINNING, it all came down to sea shells. The earliest settlers were drawn to this area by an abundance of shellfish in the bay. But this fact was lost for millennia – until a chance encounter by a mollusc expert on a train. The American zoologist Edward S. Morse (1838–1925) came to Japan in search of details of western Pacific variants of his beloved brachiopods, and happened to be looking out of the window of his train in 1877 as it passed through the village of Ōmori. Identifying a nearby hillock as an ancient shell midden (because, it is implied, the railway cutting had sliced through it), he tried to contain his excitement over the ensuing months, seemingly in the belief that the world was full of competing mollusc experts desperate to excavate it. Having obtained permission from the railway managers to walk along the line *but not to dig*, he returned with students from Tokyo Imperial University. Pawing through the upper layers with their bare hands, they soon uncovered worked bones, a clay tablet and 'a large collection of unique forms of pottery'. Morse was 'frantic with delight', sure that he had uncovered 'evidence of the aborigines of the country'. Someone living 5,000 years ago had been filching shellfish out of the mud of Tokyo Bay, slurping up the contents and throwing the shells on this trash heap.

Before long, Morse was back with labourers, hoes and trowels, gouging a chunk out of the hillside in a frenzied two-hour effort, before backfilling the hole, smoothing the surface and scarpering before the stationmaster caught him. Today, nobody remembers the unsanctioned nature of his exploration – they only remember his description of the distinctive patterns in the shards he uncovered, which looked as if some ancient potter had pushed a rope against the still-drying clay to make decorative dents. Morse called these shards 'cord-marked', and it is the Japanese translation of his description, *Jōmon*, that is used to describe the Japanese archaeological period from 14,000 BC to around 300 BC.

Until the great drainings and landfills of the Shōguns' time, much of the Tokyo area comprised tidal marshes. Several rivers – including the Sumida, Tama, Tone and Edo – dumped their waters in the bay, across acres of mudflats teeming with red-crowned cranes, plovers and kestrels. In some places, the ground was higher, thanks to forgotten volcanic eruptions that had deposited a 20-metre-thick layer of red clay: the Kantō loam stratum.

The ground was unsteady. For thousands of years, much of Tokyo's rainfall came packed into short torrential monsoon seasons, which carved deep gullies and sinkholes in the mudflats. Today, these seasonal ghost rivers form the tracks of hidden storm drains, or the pathways of twisting streets.

Sometimes, they would be completely flooded, the waters washing inland as far as the Musashino Terrace, a tableland of higher ground formed by fluvial deposits from the Tama River. The Musashino heights slope down towards the sea from 190 metres above sea level in the hinterland to the edge of what were once the mudflats, where they drop down a 20-metre-high ridge. In more recent times, the difference between these low-lying and higher areas would worm its way into Tokyo place names. The high ground was **Yamanote** ('Hillwards'), best known today for lending its name to the train line that originally connected two of its townships. The coastal area was **Umite** ('Seawards'), although it is most often known today as **Shitamachi** or the 'Low City'.

During the last Ice Age, the waters receded, turning the mudflats into a more inviting place for settlement. Hunters came through, chasing down the last of the native elephants and deer. About 9,500 years ago, one of these groups of wanderers made the area their home. Centuries of dryness served to harden the formerly soft clay, so that when the waters rose again, they sloshed against fingers of land reaching out into the bay – perfect perches from which to catch fish or gather clams and cockles. Morse's middens were the refuse of such spring and summer activities, when seafood was the most crucial part of the locals' diet. In the autumn, they would give up on the coast and venture back into the forests in search of acorns, chestnuts and wild grapes. In the winter, they would hunt.

Modern archaeologists have suggested that the shell-fish were the key. Jōmon peoples on the eastern side of Japan, particularly in the Tokyo region with its vast, shel-tered, muddy bay, had substantially better access to food than those in western Japan, whose diet relied far more heavily on acorns. But even the eastern Jōmon people needed somewhere to store their nuts and berries for the lean times, which is what led them to develop their pottery. Over the centuries, their hunter-gatherer lifestyle became increasingly sedentary as they learned to encour-age the formerly 'wild' foods to grow closer to home. Not for the last time, they appear to have been swamped by newcomers bearing new technologies – metalwork and rice seeds – arriving from the mainland and walking up the coast. Morse ruffled some feathers in the nineteenth century by suggesting that the Jōmon people were 'pre-Ainu', and that the ancestors of the modern Japanese had forced aborigines out of their homeland and ever further to the north, where the last of their descendants formed the natives of distant Hokkaidō. In our time, this supposition is widely understood to be very likely, but it was a shock to the people of the day.

The Yayoi People

The Jōmon people's successors turned into farmers, clearing forest areas with their new iron tools, and potters whose downtime was spent making not only functional items for storage, but also flare-skirted figurines, the *haniwa*, for use in funeral rituals. This Iron Age culture, flourishing from 300 BC to AD 300, derives its name from another Tokyo dig, undertaken by the generation of Japanese students that had been trained by Morse. Carrying on his work in 1884, they poked around their own university campus, uncovering a collection of pottery amid the residential construction then underway on nearby Yayoi Hill. The ornate, alien ceramics style, posited to have been undertaken by local potters to meet demand from newly arrived conquerors from the mainland, came to be known as Yayoi.

The fast-flowing Tama River was ideally suited for rice farming, providing a copious supply of fresh water that could be directed to nearby fields. But it was also flood-prone. Large-scale irrigation works, impossible to organise among individual landholders, were required to keep the Tama tame, but paid rich agricultural dividends when the work was done. Hence, the region seems to have become the centre of a particularly powerful polity during the Dark Ages. As to who these people were, today we only have the evidence of their graves and a few scattered references to their legends, preserved in ancient poems.

There are some 60 grave mounds located in the middle and lower reaches of the Tama River as it flows into what is now the Tokyo suburbs, until it reaches the sea near what is now Haneda Airport. One of these tombs, named Hōrai-san and located right next to Tamagawa station, is Tokyo's oldest, dating from the fourth century. It shares its name with many similar graves around Japan, and indeed in Japanese garden design, where *hōrai-san* (treasure mountain) is used to denote a hillock or islet in a decorative pond. As in many other cultures, regardless of prohibitions from the government, the prospect that ancient graves might contain treasure has often been a lure for would-be tomb raiders.

Not far from the course of the Tama River, **Todoroki** ('Roaring') station in the western suburbs derived its name from the waterfall that once thundered into a nearby tributary, the Yazawa. Today, the great fall is a diminished version of its former self, bubbling into a stream that flows through a 1.2-kilometre valley – one of the last remaining in modern Tokyo. Where all the other dales have been filled and hills flattened, Todoroki Gorge is a charming reminder of Tokyo's primeval past. The trees overhead block out much of the cityscape, and the gentle Yazawa brook moves briskly along, throwing off a welcome cloud of mist in the hot summer months.

Only a couple of blocks away is Nogemachi Park, the site of a fifth-century tomb mound representative of the departed Kōfun culture. The mound's outskirts are circled by smooth stones lifted from the nearby Tama River, once interspersed with the sophisticated, flare-skirted *haniwa* figurines. When excavated, the Noge tomb was found to contain three coffins, one in stone and two in wood, along with iron arrowheads, swords and adornments. It was plainly the resting place of a major chieftain, worthy enough or martial enough to have acquired some of the hallowed, much-prized bronze mirrors that were sent to Japan from distant China as diplomatic gifts, and that slowly spread out among the local tribes as bridal dowries and spoils of war.

The imperial heartland of Japan was far to the south, in Kyōto. The wide area of flat ground that would eventually become the Tokyo region derived its name – *Kantō*, 'Beyond the Barriers' – from being on the very edge of civilisation, and beyond three key military checkpoints on the road north. Some even called it *Tōgoku*, 'the Eastern Country', as if it were a separate realm.

The Kantō region possessed immense potential for development, but was a marshy borderland, a testing ground for younger sons and discredited courtiers. Whenever plagues, famines or other natural disasters brought the population of Japan down, the Kantō region was the site of an ebbing tide of settlement; there is evidence in some places of multiple clearances, of forests being chopped down for fields and then re-cleared, as if later generations returned to a site that had formerly been left derelict.

At some point in the Dark Ages, the Kantō region attracted a new group of settlers. During and after the collapse of a kingdom on the mainland, Japan was flooded with Korean immigrants and refugees. I use both of these terms because the migration was liable to have spanned many years, including both canny aristocrats and their entourages quitting while they were ahead and seeking asylum with their relatives, and unfortunate commoners piling into the last boats out of a burning harbour. Certain clans among these new settlers were co-opted into the imperial court, but with estimates ranging as high as a million new arrivals, there cannot possibly have been space for them all in the civilised south. A number, it seems, were pointed northwards at the Kantō plain and told that this land was theirs for the taking, leading to an unchronicled movement of people into the area. The first real evidence of this comes in AD 628, when two brothers fishing by the river are supposed to have pulled a golden statuette of Kannon (in Chinese, Guan Yin), the Goddess of Mercy, out of the muddy water. Installed in the local landlord's mansion, and soon hidden behind layer after layer of protective cloth and concealing screens, it eventually became the centrepiece of a temple on Akasaka (the 'Red Slope'). These stories do not arise out of nowhere – a temple implies worshippers and worshippers suggest residents. It may well have been that the settlers who entered this region in the seventh century were those Korean exiles, fleeing a war on the mainland and relocating to the edges of the Japanese state.

One of them is thought to have been buried in a keyhole-shaped tomb at the water's edge. It is now almost a mile from the sea, and so thickly overgrown with trees that few visitors even notice it, even though it is right in front of their noses. The Maruyama ('Round Mountain') tumulus is the largest keyhole tomb in the Tokyo area at 170 metres long and 8 metres high, which makes it small by the standards of the giant tombs in the south, but still liable to be the resting place of an important figure. The top was flattened in the samurai era to make room for a teahouse, but the site was spared further damage when it became the centre of the Shōguns' graveyard. Today, it is an inconspicuous hill in Shiba Park at the foot of Tokyo Tower, its distinctive shape entirely blurred and obscured by all the foliage. Nobody knows for sure who is buried there.

The Flying Head

In 646, the upland region was named Musashi – the 'Weapons Storehouse'. This, however, seems to have been a garbling of an old Ainu word for the same area, *muzasi*, which may have meant 'wilderness of weeds'. Sometimes it was known simply as Bushū, 'Warlands', signifying the long, long line of generations pushing and shoving among the colonists who arrived there, and the forgotten aboriginals they supplanted, assimilated or killed.

The first famous – or, rather, infamous – figure in the Tokyo region was Taira Masakado, who led a brief insurrection. A fifth-generation descendant of an Emperor, Masakado was one of the minor nobility who cluttered the courtyards and cloisters of Kyōto, the imperial capital. He served as a youth in the court and, like many of his fellow surplus lordlings, was packed off to the north for a long retirement as a country gentleman. Unfortunately for everybody involved, the Kantō plain was home to not one single landowner, but a whole cluster of forts and homesteads of similar figures, many of whom had elaborate allegiances and vendettas that snaked back to the capital. These were sure to spring to life on the borderlands if someone said the wrong thing, claimed to own a particular well or pastured their horses on the wrong piece of ground.

Masakado's clan, the Taira, had been artificially formed by lopping off entire branches of the imperial family. Masakado's quarrels with his neighbours, which erupted into open battle in AD 935 and rebellion in AD 939, were partly born from the fact that the rival Minamoto clan *also* comprised the descendants of past Emperors and their concubines, edged out of the cosy court life by sheer pressure of numbers. But Masakado also got into fights with other Taira, and soon began seizing the territory of others. Eventually, he took over a government base in a nearby province, elevating his action from the realm of a local squabble into a treasonous attack on the Emperor's authority. Masakado was proclaimed a public enemy and targeted by vengeful samurai, and his brief reign as the nominal overlord of an independent Kantō was brought crashing down in early AD 940, barely a couple of months after it had been declared.

There, you might think, it all could have ended, but Masakado's story would grow with the telling, particularly in later centuries when the Taira–Minamoto enmity escalated into full-scale civil war. Masakado became a much-studied precedent, either for rebelling against the Emperor or for putting down such rebels. Thanks to an enduring book about his life, he became something of a bad-boys' rent-a-quote in the centuries that followed, not least with his blunt statement that 'the people of this world will always anoint their sovereigns through victory in combat'. Perhaps in an attempt to stop anyone imitating him, a coda was swiftly arranged in which the spirit of Masakado was subjected to eternal torture in the hereafter:

> While I dwelt on the earthly plane, I did not one good deed, and for this wicked karma I spin through evil incarnations. At this moment 15,000 souls indict me – how painful that is. When I did evil deeds, I gathered followers and through them committed my crimes. But on the day of judgement, I took on all my sins, and suffer alone.

Masakado's supposed punishment in the afterlife seems to have been designed as an attempt to clear the records and settle all disputes. Taira and Minamoto alike were exhorted to get along on the borderlands, safe in the knowledge that any crimes that had been committed against one another were being exorcised in the next life through the eternal torment of Masakado, whose body was being eternally pierced by sword-leaf trees, and whose liver was roasting over hot coals. In the twilight of the samurai, where the entire caste paid lip service to ideas of honour and nobility, there was a certain cheeky sheen to the days of Masakado, when well-situated forts and a lack of siege capabilities made everyone favour the ambush as a means of dealing with opponents before they realised a war was underway. But Masakado's legend was already growing in the years immediately after his death.

There were stories that he was all but invulnerable, save for a single weak spot – the stories differed on this point, but it was said to possibly be in one of his eyes, which had two pupils, or on the top of his head, where his serpent-mother had failed to lick him to Achilles-like indestructability. The already-credulous superstitions of the Middle Ages became interwoven with his legend. Stories told of a plague of butterflies before his rebellion, the imperial capital being wracked by a five-day series of earthquakes, and rainbows breaking out in 20 simultaneous places around Kyōto. His daughter, Takiyasha, it was said, lived on as a witch in the ruins of his castle, experimenting with dark sorceries to avenge his death, and briefly becoming the leader of an army of frogs – the word for frog in Japanese is *kaeru*, which also means 'return'.

Masakado's brief reign of terror having been brought to an end, the stories say, his disembodied head was brought to Kyōto, where it was hung on a tree near the East Market for display. And that, one would hope, would be the end of it – except the head refused to rot, allegedly howled during the night and was heard by some witnesses to be speaking, demanding to know where its body was.

Eventually, the errant head flew away. A temple in

Gifu marks the spot where a local warrior shot at it with an arrow, and then it was on the move again, eventually coming to rest in the obscure village of **Shibazaki** ('Brushwood Ridge'). The villagers washed it and buried it with full honours, hoping to dispel any curse, although before long, the shrine where it rested was subjected to lightning strikes and strange apparitions. The grave mound (*kubizuka*) over Masakado's head became associated in the centuries that followed with malevolence and misfortune. As long as it was carefully maintained, the inscriptions on its stone stela would keep Masakado's dark powers in check, but whenever bad luck struck the people of the surrounding area, it was sure to be associated with him.

The village of Shibazaki, needless to say, ended up incorporated within Tokyo. Urban myths associated with Masakado would crop up throughout the centuries that followed – you have not seen the last of him in this book.

The court in Kyōto considered itself well rid of Masakado, given that he was banished to a ghastly province that no right-minded nobleman would ever want to visit. The Kyōto nobleman favoured the capital's gentle plain contained within a shield-wall of green mountains; the very idea of Kantō's vast flatlands seemed preposterous and ugly. In 1020, the young Lady Sarashina crossed what is now the Sumida River, and reported in her diary that the reeds there were so tall that they obscured not only her outrider horsemen, but also the tips of their long bows. Indeed, for much of the early Middle Ages, the area that would become Tokyo remained uncleared – a tangle of grass, trees and reeds, with little high ground from which an observer could get the lay of the land.

By the eleventh century, the region was succumbing to new colonists. The **Shibuya** ('Bitter Valley') family constructed a stronghold on the ground that still retains their name to this day. A hundred years later, within sight of the smoke from the Shibuya cooking fires, the samurai Chichibu Shigetsugu built himself a fort on a hill overlooking the estuary, near the site of what is now the Imperial Palace. A plain-spoken man not given to flights of whimsy, he named it Edo – 'Estuary'.

2

The Growth of a City: 1200s–1657

CENTRALLY LOCATED, handy for public transport and a mandatory inclusion on a one-day tour of Tokyo, the Imperial Palace is a sure-fire attraction for the average tourist. It is, however, not the kind of place you can just walk into. A high wall shuts off much of the core, creating a primal patch of green in the centre of town, reminiscent of the ancient tumuli that scatter south Japan, untouched by the rush of the modern world.

It once occupied a much larger area. Today, the walled enclosure is a mere 7.41 square kilometres, although popular myth claimed in the 1980s boom-time that it was real estate worth more than all of California. Parts of what were once the outlying palace grounds were repurposed during the Second World War to form a public park and the area where the national **Budōkan** ('Martial Arts Hall') stadium now stands.

Visitors can still wander the picturesque eastern grounds, examining the extant foundations of formerly imposing towers and the ruins of the keep that was once the Shōgun's castle. Before Tokyo was home to Emperors, it was the power base of the Emperors' leading general, a man so powerful that some foreign visitors mistook him for the 'king' of Japan. And it was here, in what was once his realm, that two of the Shōgun's men got into a fateful scuffle.

A sign marks the spot that once was the Pine Corridor, where in 1701 the young Lord Asano, pushed that little bit too far by the snooty official Kira, drew his sword and struck his tormentor. Even the samurai were bound by rules of propriety – Asano had already lost at the moment he reached for his weapon. He was sentenced to death, although his 47 most loyal henchmen vengefully murdered Kira two years later and left his head on Asano's grave before committing mass suicide. The tale of the 47 *rōnin* (masterless samurai) was one of the most scandalous incidents of the samurai era, but was slyly admired by many an armchair general. Everybody in eighteenth-century Japan had an opinion about the etiquette of fights and vendettas, and the myriad 'what-ifs' of the sequence of events. What if Asano had just held his cool? What if Asano had killed Kira? What if Kira had died of natural causes before the *rōnin* could avenge their master? What if the *rōnin* had not committed suicide, but simply gone on the run?

You are unlikely to have the opportunity to see the inner precincts, where the Emperor himself still resides. Only on 2 January each year is the public granted access to the inner gardens, where loyal subjects might hope to catch a glimpse of the Emperor waving from a balcony. The rest of the time, tourists can come no closer than the other side of the moat, by the two gentle arches of the stone access bridge popularly known as Meganebashi ('Spectacles Bridge') for the effect created by the reflection of its span in the waters below. Beyond it are the high walls, and the few towers that still evoke the days when this was Edo Castle, even though many of the extant buildings only date from 1970.

I have watched the tourist coaches disgorge their contents outside the palace entrance, abandoning their charges for 20 minutes of snacks and selfies, uncaring that there isn't a whole lot to see here. That, however, is part of the point. This patch of green was where the estuary fort first arose, diverting a local river to create the first moat, and causing the old inlet to silt up. A forest of black pines in the park, ignored by most visitors as just a bunch of trees, was planted in 1888 to mark the boggy ground that was once the water's edge – today, it is a kilometre's walk from Tokyo Bay.

Inevitably, the crowds shuffle over to the bronze statue in the corner of the parkland. To most, it is just a samurai on a horse. In fact, it is Kusunoki Masashige (1294–1336), one of the most famous warriors of yesteryear. He is in full armour, wrestling his mount in what appears to be a turn, stern with resolve and fearlessness. Kusunoki is a figure of legendary renown, a henchman who arrived in the life of the beleaguered Emperor Go-Daigo after the sovereign dreamed divine assistance was coming his way. In a brief military career lasting just five years, Kusunoki held two critical forts for his lord for as long as possible, and was rewarded with the governorship of two provinces. When the Ashikaga family turned on the Emperor, it was Kusunoki who advised him to hole up with the monks on Mount Hiei, only for the inexperienced Emperor to insist on meeting his foes head-on. On the field, Kusunoki pleaded with his Emperor to adopt any one of several tactics that might give them the upper hand, but he was overruled.

Knowing it was going to be a disaster, and certain that it would spell his own death, Kusunoki nevertheless did as he was told. His battalion charged against impossible odds, and was soon hacked down from 700 to just 50 men. As their foes closed in, Kusunoki prepared a counter-attack, sure that it would kill him. The statue shows him in the moment that he wheels his mount to lead a suicidal charge, when, as legend has it, his similarly loyal brother shouted the fateful words: 'Would that I had seven lives to give for my country!'

I don't think Kusunoki ever made it this far north. His dukedoms were in the Ōsaka area, as were his most famous victories. He fell in battle at Minatogawa, in what is now a Kobe suburb, but for the last century his statue has become an enduring landmark in Tokyo, a town that did not even exist during his lifetime. Kusunoki's rise to fame was a symptom of the Tokugawa era's constant debates on loyalty. Once written off as a flunky to a hapless pretender, he was reimagined during the long early modern peace as a paragon of obedience. As Japan modernised, the story of his refusal to countermand his father figure became a staple of children's schoolbooks, which made a meal of his stoic farewell to his own son. Japanese schoolchildren in the pre-war era got to learn a song about it, and Kusunoki became such an icon that he was officially incorporated into the honours system, posthumously awarded an imperial rank in 1880.

The statue of him, a group effort by four sculptors in the style of similar Victorian-era monuments in distant Europe, was raised in 1897 on the outskirts of the Imperial Palace, all the better to remind visiting subjects of the approved mode of conduct when told what to do by an Emperor. Inevitably, during the Second World War, Kusunoki's suicidal loyalty became a touchstone for the kamikaze pilots. Considering its military associations, it is surprising indeed that Kusunoki's statue survived to the present day, but his character as a noble figure through the ages seems to have well and truly trumped any associations he may have had with the wartime regime.

Ieyasu's Folly

The Kantō area was a patchwork of landholdings, passed back and forth between the samurai in Japan's various civil conflicts. Shigetsugu's son Shigenaga, now using the surname Edo after his main domain, was awarded several other patches of real estate in 1180, after his well-timed switch in sides made him a useful figure for the Minamoto clan. One of these was **Kitami**, written with the characters for 'many lucky views', but thought to have originally been an old Ainu term for 'flat, wooded area'. The Edo clan did not fare particularly well in the shunts and double-deals of Japan's samurai wars. They briefly flourished as the landlords of whatever hapless fishermen lived near their stronghold, before fading into the tapestry of flunkies and hangers-on of the warlord era's more recognisable names. Edo was one of several strongholds dotted around the plain, although the region remained dangerous for the unwary traveller. **Dōgenzaka** ('Dōgen's Slope') on the edge of Shibuya, derives its modern name from that of a medieval bandit who would lay in wait for travellers as they passed through the valley.

By 1457, the Edo family had been ordered off the land that gave them their name, drifting off to their second home in Kitami – the Keigen-ji temple in the western suburbs still has the memorial tablets of several clan members. They handed their Edo land over to Ōta Dōkan, although to hear local legend tell of the change-over, it was less about a shuffling of minions than it was a fantasy epic. The goddess Benten, so it was said, leapt from the waters in the form of a *konoshiro* fish, which the superstitious Ōta took as a message from the fates: *kono shiro* means 'this castle'. There was a patch of high ground nearby, and that is where he decided to build.

If the story is true, Ōta must have been extraordinarily thick to require such guidance, because his bamboo stockade and wooden fortifications were placed on top of the ones already put there by the Edo family. Edo Castle not only stood in a good, defensible position, but it had a commanding view of several nearby rivers (one of which was diverted to form its moat), as well as **Hibiya** ('Sunny Dale' – although this is a probably a modern spin, and *hibi* likely referred to oyster traps in the shallows), a nearby inlet where a quay had been built through the soft ground of the wetlands. Boats could safely anchor away from the open estuary, and during Ōta's brief tenure the Hibiya anchorage began to transform into a thriving commercial harbour.

Ōta was not an educated man. Caught in the rain while out hunting, he legendarily knocked on the door of a farmer and asked for a straw raincoat. The woman who answered the door mysteriously handed him a *yamabuki*, a kind of yellow rose. Baffled, Ōta turned away and sloshed home through the storm. It was one of his henchmen that pointed out to him that the whole thing had been a poetic joke – an allusion to a medieval poem in which a prince laments that even the yellow rose has a raincoat, but not him. Ōta resolved to learn more about this poetry lark, and would eventually write his own verses. Some of them were not very good – his death poem, in particular, is a strangled mess of conditional clauses and double negatives – but while he was the lord of the castle he did come up with something that endured for centuries. Standing in the very centre of what would one day become Tokyo, he proclaimed:

This abode of mine
Sits by the pine groves
On the blue sea
And from its humble roof
The sight of soaring Fuji

Five hundred years after his death, these words would be dragged up in a mayoral election campaign, when a candidate pointed out that it was no longer all that easy to see Mount Fuji from the castle, because of all the air pollution. Ōta's poem would become the inspiration for one of Tokyo's first clean-air campaigns.

But the Ōta clan, like the Edo family before it, did not fare well. Ōta himself was killed over intrigues among the samurai. Although his clan would endure as minor nobles for the next three centuries, they were shuffled around from place to place. The castle that Ōta had requisitioned from the Edo clan was left to fall into ruin, and after a century its only occupants were crows. The Hibiya inlet silted up, turning into yet another patch of boggy ground.

Everything changed in 1590 when, in the last decade of the prolonged samurai wars, the double-crosses and double-deals finally came to an end. On a campaign against the Hōjō clan, the warlord Hideyoshi made an unexpected offer to his lieutenant Tokugawa Ieyasu. If Ieyasu were to give up his multiple domains in the south, Hideyoshi would give him all the captured territories of the Hōjō, amounting to much of the Kantō plain. It was likely to have been a political move designed to neutralise a potential threat, depriving Ieyasu of his home base and lumbering him with former enemy territory, populated by resentful ex-Hōjō samurai. Ieyasu, however, accepted the offer. He moved into the ruined castle on the estuary, and devoted himself to consolidating his new holdings. While Hideyoshi remained occupied with mop-up operations in the south and an ill-fated campaign in Korea, Ieyasu was sitting pretty on the Kantō plain, suitably distant from most of the military requisition orders, and insulated from any attacks. As one Japanese proverb puts it: 'Ieyasu won the empire by retreating.'

Hindsight accords Ieyasu with incredible powers of prophecy – the ability to visualise the city that Tokyo would become. Certainly, its geography offered some distinct advantages, sitting pretty at the foot of the Kantō plain, with access to both the sea and the Tone River – which, of all the spaghetti of streams that reached the sea at Edo, stretched the furthest into the hinterland, and remains Japan's second longest river. Perhaps more importantly for its long-term survival, the site of Edo was shielded from the ocean by the great curve of the Bōsō Peninsula, leaving it less prone to storm damage than other coastal cities.

As Hideyoshi's faction inevitably fell apart, and the warlords squabbled over who spoke for his son, Ieyasu became the primary figure in the new power games. In the year 1600, he was victorious at the Battle of Sekigahara, a watershed moment in Japanese history that would fix the positions and relationships of the samurai houses for more than two centuries. Anyone who was on Ieyasu's side at the Battle of Sekigahara would become a trusted noble in his new order, more often than not, locked into a domain that controlled a crucial transit point, or given control of a lucrative estate. Anyone who only submitted to Ieyasu's authority after the Battle of Sekigahara was over was given a lesser status, shunted into low-yield domains or given far-off positions on difficult terrain or with fractious locals. All of them, however, were expected to travel to Ieyasu's headquarters for meetings, consultations and displays of loyalty. All roads soon led to Edo.

By 1603, Ieyasu had surpassed his former boss Hideyoshi, successfully arranging for himself to be named Shōgun. Originally an extraordinary military appointment, delegating imperial authority to a general in a frontier war, the title had come to signify whoever it was that held the true power in Japan. The Shōgun ruled

Japan in the Emperor's name, and although Ieyasu was by no means the first to hold the position, his complete victory at Sekigahara, and the swift steps he took to head off any likely competition, ensured that he and his Tokugawa descendants would rule Japan for the next 250 years. The most draconian and far-reaching element of their reign was the expulsion of Europeans, in order to avoid the political and religious interference that had characterised some of the wars of the previous century. The Sakoku ('Locked Country') Edicts threw out anyone with more than one foreign grandparent, corralling the remaining outsiders, including merchants from China, into a couple of tiny enclaves in the far south. Until the 1850s, Tokyo was a European-free zone, except for an annual glimpse of Dutch merchants coming to pay homage to the Shōgun from their ghetto in Nagasaki. Left practically to its own devices for 250 years, Japan developed along its own course, untroubled by events in the outside world. Knowledge of the world outside was filtered through an elite of special experts, known as scholars of 'Dutch studies'.

Kyōto in the south remained officially the capital, since that was where the figurehead Emperor resided, although it became increasingly marginalised and impoverished as all the real players migrated to Ieyasu's stronghold. Edo, with both its commanding position on the Kantō plain and the roads that connected it to the rest of the country, was the true centre of power. The expanding Edo Castle grounds forced some relocations, not for the last time, starting with Ieyasu's favourite shrine, which was moved to nearby Kanda. It is still called the **Kanda Shrine** (see Gazetteer: Chiyoda), even though it was moved again in 1616 to what is now Akihabara.

In 1603, the year of Ieyasu's victory, a river crossing was built at Nihonbashi ('Japan Bridge'). If there was a commercial centre to the city, this was it – all road distances to the capital were measured to Nihonbashi, which soon became a thriving trade district under the stewardship of the Mitsui family. The scale, however, started very small; early Edo was no more than a couple of miles across.

Edo Castle, now the Imperial Palace, is much changed today from its seventeenth-century appearance, although some element of its bulk is preserved in the massive walls and ramparts. The castle's designers would claim it accorded exactly to the principles of feng shui, although this was only supported by a series of outrageous fudges, sufficient to make any geomancer tear his hair out. The most infamous was the reorientation of Ōtemon (the main gate) to face east instead of south, in order to put Mount Fuji in the west at the 'back' of the castle. Others were less immediately obvious, such as a scheme to encourage temples to the north-east in order to serve as a spiritual rampart against an inauspicious direction – there were 36 of them by 1700, packing what is now Ueno with pilgrims and priests until 16% of the city was holy ground of some description.

The road into town required a protective garrison, leading to the establishment of a small barracks out near Seizoroi-zaka ('Mustering Hill'). A number of mansions and residences for samurai retainers sprang up amid the fields, which were irrigated with the aid of a water-wheel on the nearby Shibuya River. The land, however, was never all that rewarding, leading to many stories of impoverished local farmers beseeching the gods for better harvests or beneficial rains. The area became known simply as **Harajuku** ('Field Lodge').

One of the outlying villages incorporated in the long, low sprawl was Shibazaki, the fabled resting place of the head of the rebel samurai Masakado. His grave mound ended up walled within the gardens of the mansion of the Sakai samurai family. It was a rather imposing hillock, some 7 metres high and 30 metres around, set in a peaceful garden beside a lily pond. Before it stood a large plinth, upon which was a stone stela proclaiming Masakado's Buddhist name, and hence thwarting his evil designs on the human world.

In 1634, expansion work on Edo Castle and its massive moat forced many locals out of their homes. The mansions of the most trusted and valued *daimyō* (feudal lords, literally meaning 'great names') now sat in **Marunouchi** ('Within the Moat'), the prime new real estate that sat behind the outermost protective ditch, but the former inhabitants had to find new locations. Several shrines and temples dismantled their wooden buildings, packed up their finery and statuary, and reassembled them further afield in the farming village of **Yotsuya** ('Four Valleys'), where a watchtower had been constructed to overlook the road into town. As a centre for worship and interment, Yotsuya soon gained an outer community of tradesmen and services. It flourished all the more after 1657, when much of Edo was destroyed in a fire, but Yotsuya remained untouched, becoming a nucleus for urban renewal. The nearby area became known as **Shinjuku** (the 'New Lodge').

Alternate Attendance

A feature of Ieyasu's reign, and of all subsequent Tokugawa rulers, was a requirement for the feudal lords to be at his beck and call at his headquarters – usually one year on, one year off, although exceptions were made for outlying lords who had further to travel. Each domain was required to set up an embassy of sorts in Edo, inevitably comprising a large walled mansion, sufficient to keep the feudal lord in a suitable manner, which in turn would require a significant entourage of servants and attendants. Even when the lord himself was not personally present, he was obliged to leave his family members behind – hostages in all but name.

This practice became known as *sankin kōtai* (alternate attendance), and it was to play a significant part in shaping the culture of Japan as a whole, and Edo in particular. Some 70% of Edo's buildings were residences for these samurai. Any domain worth its salt would probably have at least three mansions – an upper one close to the castle; a middle residence further afield, liable to be used by retired lords or the family of an absent ruler; and a lower residence out towards the countryside, to be used as something of a summer retreat. The land such mansions were built on belonged to the Shōgun and could be redistributed at will. The mansions themselves, however, were the financial responsibility of their occupants, and drained a huge amount of money from each domain. Not for the last time in Tokyo architecture, these lords' residences were strictly functional with a front-end flourish – anonymous walls and drab roofs gave them a grim, barrack-like look from the outside, which was always a wise move when one could never predict the timing of the next Shōgunal austerity drive. The backstreets around them were similarly functional. Designed as firebreaks, they were usually deserted, with no space for private residences and no passing trade for shops. The gates, however, would become the load-bearers of all the frustrated and suppressed gaudiness, single points of access to the inner compound, facing a public street and hence the domain's single chance to advertise its prowess, power and prestige to passers-by. The mansion gates were brightly coloured, often in fierce red or brilliant orange, with upswept roofs and lacquered decorations.

The upkeep of several mansions with their staff was coupled with the immense expense of travelling to and from Edo in long processions of outlying watchmen, porters, bearers and samurai. Such entourages were a regular sight in Tokugawa Japan, clogging the roads into Edo and fostering a thriving 'tourist' industry of roadside inns that could put up dozens of demanding guests. Feudal lords were responsible for maintaining the roads in their domains for the benefit of any other samurai passing through, dragging the entire country into a cycle of expenditure and make-work tasks. Constantine Vaporis, a historian of the *sankin kōtai* phenomenon, estimates that the entire enterprise was sure to drain half to three-quarters of each domain's annual budget. Since attendance alternated for different domains on different dates, up to two-thirds of the population of Edo would cycle out each year, heading home after their tours of duty, to be replaced by another set of domain lords. The city that this created began as an anonymous military camp, with women heavily outnumbered by men, and a placeless, transient culture. Soon, however, an Edo mindset began to form among the permanent residents drawn to the city to provide for the needs of its fluctuating population of samurai.

An entire generation of young samurai was reared in the ever-changing, ever-growing metropolis. Some, undoubtedly, dreaded the day that they had to begin the march to the Shōgun's ghastly, smelly, sprawling conurbation. But others looked forward to the opportunities for entertainment and adventure in such a cosmopolitan place. Within a couple of generations – by 1640, when Edo Castle was pronounced complete – Edo was the place where every feudal lord and noblewoman had effectively grown up.

The rapid construction of mansions for nobles from

every corner of Japan soon began to transform the landscape. The houses, their attendant outbuildings and the followers, hangers-on and peripheral services took up even more space. Saddlers, leatherworkers, blacksmiths, merchants and shops crowded out the hard ground. The marshes and rice paddies were drained away, their edges etched with channels to carry away the surplus water, creating new squares of firmer ground but also cutting, re-cutting and re-re-cutting the watercourses that had previously tumbled freely across the mudflats and wetlands. It was hence only at this point, as the Tokugawa city began to form, that names were attached to certain watercourses as they were forced into new or deeper channels, or locked into stone-walled canals. Sometimes the names would stick; other times, a watercourse would have several titles, depending on what part of the city its observer was in. Either the designation would be fixed when a town official drew a map and needed to pick a single name, or the watercourse itself would be filled, merged or diverted by yet another land reclamation scheme. The Sumida River, for example – now considered to be the main waterway of modern Tokyo, and famous from many a song and poem – is not even mentioned in accounts of the area before this period, nor does it show up on early maps. Look at several city plans over a period of time, however, and the Sumida starts to manifest before your eyes, like raindrops running and conjoining on a window pane.

Edo was very much a water city, criss-crossed with canals for freight and transportation. Its streets and alleys were too narrow for wheeled carts. Most transportation was still by porter or bearer, with the occasional rider on horseback. For everybody else, the quickest and most effective way to travel around the city was by boat. The Kanda River all but disappeared in a series of re-routings

that created the moats of Edo Castle, but also in the construction of a drinking water supply system, dispersing
its contents through 3,600 aqueducts, some of them little
more than bamboo tubes. However, Edo grew so fast that
a second system was required by the 1650s, leading to
an 80-kilometre network that diverted waters from the
Tama River into the city. Government directives forbade
the ejection of waste material into the waters of the city,
creating a flourishing sub-industry of dunny men, who
would wheel their carts around the city offering to buy
excrement to use as fertiliser. Every day, their carts would
cause a stinky traffic jam on the road junction out of the
city towards the outlying farms, leading to a nickname
that Shinjuku realtors would prefer to forget – 'the arse
of Edo'. Despite such efforts to make the city liveable, the
court aristocrats of the south still looked upon it with
snooty derision. '*Edo wa tenka no hakidamari,*' they
would tell each other. 'Edo is the Emperor's trash heap.'

The Flowers of Edo

The Sumida River was sure to rise every year, either
directly endangering the Low City slums or increasing
the spread of rat- or fly-borne diseases. But in a town of
close-packed wooden houses, every one with a hearth,
the greatest danger was fire. Periodic conflagrations
destroyed entire districts of the city, and could be kicked
off by a single errant spark. The most astonishing was the
Meireki Fire of January 1657 (like many such events, it
derives its name from the reign-period in which it took
place), which legendarily began, like some horror movie
foreshadowing, with a haunted kimono.

This article of clothing had been owned by three girls
in succession, every one of whom had met with a sudden
death. Believing the kimono to be cursed, its new owners

ordered it to be burned at a Buddhist temple. A gust of strong wind lifted up fragments of the burning silk and deposited them on a temple roof, which soon caught alight. The flames jumped from temple to tavern, over bridges and storehouses, burning down six entire districts. In the chaos, a second fire started, perhaps from a neglected cooking stove or a dropped tobacco pipe. With the populace already distracted by the first fire, the second raged through the samurai district, burning alive the inmates of the city prison, and even destroying Edo Castle. Over 100,000 people, a third of the entire population, died in the two days of the Meireki Fire, not merely from the flames, but from the wintry aftermath. Even as the wreckage still smouldered, snow began to fall with mocking irony, dooming many newly homeless residents to death by hypothermia.

Fires were so commonplace and so feared that the locals did not even dare to call them what they were. With customarily poetic fatalism, they referred to them as 'the flowers of Edo'. Many houses gained rooftop crow's nests to allow the occupants to see how close nearby fires were getting. A common feature of every district was the *hinomi-yagura* (fire-watching tower), which looks to modern eyes like a pair of telegraph poles placed close enough together that the rungs of a ladder can run between them. At the top was a bell and a tiny perch no bigger than a footstool, allowing residents to peer into the next city block to see how great the risk was whenever they smelled smoke.

Eventually, Edo gained a new class of 'firemen' – although their job description was somewhat different from what one might expect. Exhibiting a certain resignation to the impossibility of putting out a fire, they instead ransacked the house, carrying out the valuables to spare them the flames. Private enterprises rather than publicly funded do-gooders, the firemen existed as multiple rival brigades, often leading to scrums of contending rescuers at any disaster scene. Standard bearers carrying the standard of a particular firemen's guild would perch as close to the burning building as possible, so that everyone could see who had arrived. Fire hoses, using a relatively meagre hand-pumped stream from the nearest canal, were intended not to dowse the flames, but to protect the firemen as they worked.

Over the years, it became apparent that the best way to protect one's business was to strike a deal with the firemen in advance, so that they were sure to come quickly in the event of trouble. In order to make allegiances clear, many businesses started to hang the standards of particular guilds over their doors. This was the origin of the decorated *noren*, the half-curtain that can still be found at the entrance to many a shop or noodle bar.

Despite the tragedies they caused, the flowers of Edo also led to many new developments. Burned-out areas were swiftly rebuilt, generating work for an entire class of carpenters and lumber merchants – a merchant not back in business within three days was regarded as an also-ran. The debris from each disaster was usually scooped up and dumped in the seaward marshes, contributing to the city's rapid expansion eastward into reclaimed land. After many fires, there were attempts at a more fire-resistant approach to urban planning, with wider streets and deliberate firebreaks between districts. However, land was at a premium, and such areas of empty ground soon filled up with bazaars, markets and fairs, creating new fire hazards in turn.

3

The Floating World: 1657–1853

INSIDE THE OTA MEMORIAL MUSEUM OF ART (see Gazetteer: Shibuya) the floors are laid with tatami mats. You take off your shoes and pad around the galleries in your socks. There are so many pictures in the collection, and many of them are so fragile beneath electric light, that the images on display are often changed three or four times a year. Every few months, the visitor is rewarded by the sight of a different set of prints and paintings – but, if you're lucky, you'll catch one in particular.

In this image, you can't see any of the figures' faces. They are all in shadow or partly obscured, even with the bright light that streams between the slats in the wooden house. Within, there are glimpses of red brocade and white skin, bodkins holding elaborate hairstyles in place, flashes of vibrant colours and warm light, at harsh odds with the grim shadows of the street outside. The museum calls it *Courtesans Showing Themselves to the Strollers through the Grille*, but this image is better known by the simpler title of *Night Scene at the Yoshiwara*. The courtesans are only half the subject; the artist has devoted even greater care to the dimly lit figures that ogle them – a group of anonymous men huddled in the darkness, hoping to catch a glimpse of the delights within. Some, perhaps, are mere tourists, who cannot possibly hope to afford a meeting with one of the women. Others might be customers, preparing for a return visit, or checking one more time before they take the plunge and spend a month's salary on a single evening. Three carry their own lanterns, sure that they will have to walk home in the forbidding dark.

The picture is a masterpiece of light and shadow, and a beautiful comment on the fleetingness of existence. The artist was a woman, Katsushika Ōi (c.1800–c.1866) and the picture is one of only a dozen that have been reliably identified as her work. There are many more extant, perhaps, but Ōi was cursed to be the daughter of Hokusai, that most famous of the artists of Japan's 'floating world'. Despite talents that could perhaps have even outmatched those of her father, she was fated to always work in his shadow. When Hokusai became old and infirm, she is believed to have 'helped' him in his studio, possibly to the extent of simply passing off her own work as his. There was a lot of money to be made in Hokusai artwork, then and now, and it is likely that many of Ōi's greatest works continue to be filed as the work of her father by curators, art dealers and experts who dare not rock the boat of attribution. Like many women of the samurai era, Ōi remained in the shadows, hiding her own light, barely visible from the public spaces of a man's world.

The Place Without Night

The sharp-eyed reader may have noticed that, with 86% of Edo given over to either the samurai or the priests that salved their consciences, there was perilously little of the city left for the working classes. Most lived in one-room apartments in the Low City, in long dormitory-like buildings with shared cooking, laundry, toilet and waste facilities. Prone to seasonal flooding from the Sumida

River, and cramped beyond belief, these forerunners of today's 'capsule hotels' offered little rat-infested respite from the heat of a Tokyo summer, and were packed closely enough to fall prey to periodic fires.

Life was better for the merchants, whose need for shopfronts and warehouse space allowed them to spread out a bit, living above their wares. The merchants were regarded as a class lower than the labourers, since they did not create anything of their own, but merely bought and sold the labours of others. But this was the central contradiction of Tokugawa life – that the samurai were the ruling class, but the merchants had all the money and the fun. Traders traded, and their business successes soon afforded them greater purchasing power. In the samurai social order, the merchants could only look down on the 'untouchable' *hinin* underclass that dealt with dead bodies – butchery, undertaking and leatherwork.

Even the samurai needed to shop for things, and demand often outgrew supply. A sword market at the base of the Tokiwa Bridge was often swamped with samurai trying to pick up suitable kit, to the extent that the merchants started to scrimp on quality, peddling 'antiques' that were in fact nearly new or only slightly foxed, and otherwise selling lower-grade products. Local slang gained the term *ohashi-mono* ('bridge thing') for old tat and fakery.

Merchants with more of an eye on the long term started to specialise in quality goods. In Edo's early days, its citizens still looked to the south for value, and it was some time before local soy sauce, silk, rice and even *sake* were considered to match the level of those made in Ōsaka. In 1673, Mitsui Takatoshi opened a kimono shop in Edo, a branch of his pre-existing business in the south. It was the place to buy the finest brocades and keep up with Kyōto fashions, and the stock eventually diversified into other dry goods. Mitsui, however, embraced the egalitarian melting pot of Edo in a way that allowed him to rapidly expand his client base and gain the trust of his customers. Other merchants continued to offer a bespoke experience, dealing with each client on a one-to-one basis, charging whatever the market would bear or conceding discounts to those with better bargaining power. They would also let their customers run up tabs, only calling for the settling of accounts twice a year or so. Mitsui, however, was having none of that. Everything in his store had a fixed price, regardless of what domain you came from or who your master was. Customers paid for silk on the spot and by the yard, while a dedicated team of tailors provided a full service to make actual clothes. Each of the 40 commodities in the store had a dedicated shop assistant who knew everything about it. The haughtier samurai might have turned their noses up at the idea, but the lower ranks loved it. Mitsui had invented the department store, and his Edo shop, which was eventually known as Mitsukoshi, would become the flagship of his corporation.

Merchants' houses gained tiled roofs less liable to catch fire, and their clothes soon became softer and more showy. Periodic clampdowns by the government attempted to limit the merchant class, forbidding certain forms of dress or consumption, and leaving the new rich of Edo permanently afraid of having their acquisitions confiscated. There were only two places where an Edo merchant might be able to truly let loose and display his wealth and status, because they were where the samurai were discouraged from going: the theatre and the brothel.

Another casualty of the Meireki Fire had been the Yoshiwara pleasure quarter, a district of brothels and bars to the east of the castle, long regarded with disapproval by the authorities. Its residents were ordered to pack up and move out to Asakusa, although this move backfired rather spectacularly. The new location was indeed further away and out of sight of the castle, and it was handily on the banks of the Sumida River, making it accessible to river taxis from all over the city. Canny locals sped up the traffic at the Takechō landing by petitioning to be allowed to build a bridge. The Shōgun assented, on the understanding that it was handy to have a solid river crossing on the road that went east and then up (the famous 'narrow road to the deep north'), without realising that the new bridge would also fast-track traffic into the pleasure quarter. The original wooden bridge proved impressively sturdy, winning a commendation from the government after it withstood heavy floods. It stayed in place for over a century, appearing in many a woodblock print from the era, evocative of the outskirts of the city, but also a pathway to erotic adventure and a counterpoint to images of the 'floating world'. The great bridge could be a symbol of seizing the day, or of the temptations of the flesh that lured the aesthete from the path of righteousness. Or, sometimes, a bridge was just a bridge.

Built in 1774, it had many names, including the 'Big River Bridge' and the 'East Bridge'. The name that eventually stuck was Azuma-bashi, which means 'East Bridge' but sounds like 'Wife Bridge', named after a nearby shrine. The toll for travellers was two small coins, but – and here we see the Shōgun having the last laugh – samurai crossed for free. While there was always money to be made from punters hurrying to the brothels and entertainments, any of the long processions of samurai from the country would have to be waved through.

Spared the complaints of the Shōgun, the locals also took the opportunity to proclaim themselves open all hours, leading to the Yoshiwara's new nickname: 'the Place Without Night'. Although the samurai authorities made a big deal of their disapproval, they were, of course, some of the sex workers' best customers. For most of its Tokugawa history, Edo retained its male-heavy population; men outnumbered women by a ratio of 2:1 in the seventeenth century, and it would take until 1845 for a 10:9 ratio of men to women to arise in the city (today, it is more like 95:100).

Unlike many other aspects of Edo life, the brothel quarter was entirely egalitarian, disregarding everything except the client's cash in hand. The establishments on offer ranged up to ridiculously high-class teahouses where well-to-do clients might mingle with women accomplished in the arts of conversation, music and dance. Lower-ranking women of the quarter populated various professions including those of 'dancers', 'tea-pourers' and women simply selling sex. The term *geisha* (artiste) was associated with educated and refined women in the early to mid-Tokugawa period, but it became degraded and abused, particularly in later generations, as upstarts grabbed the name but not the qualifications.

The highest class of Yoshiwara woman was a sight to behold, more like a gaudy battleship at sail than a human being. She would proceed with theatrical slowness, her every step a calculated, graceful dance move, her clothes flashing with bright embroidery and impeccably chosen seasonal colours in multiple enticing silken layers. Her hair (or more often, wig) was a frozen fountain of shiny lacquer, conceived in imitation of the hairstyles of the princesses of China's medieval Tang dynasty, held in place with a sunburst of bright bodkins. Such a costume required an army of assistants, and its wearer would walk attended by her entourage. The arrival of a woman like this at one's party would be a matter of excitement and awe, attracting celebrity gossip and gawpers at the door.

If this sounds like a counter-intuitive description of

the denizens of a 'brothel quarter', we might consider the implications of Edo life being so devoid of women. In some cases, females were entirely ornamental, since a substantial number of samurai preferred boys anyway – this was known euphemistically in later years as the 'Satsuma preference', after the domain in Japan's far south where Tokyo locals liked to think it was most popular. In others, sexual congress with a woman was merely the cherry on the cake, delivered after one or more tantalising evenings of conversation, party games and acts of adoration.

There were many levels in the hierarchy of Yoshiwara labourers. Beneath the celebrity performers, there were the *oiran*, adept at delivering what we might call a 'girl-friend experience'. The name is written with the characters for 'first flower', but truly derives from a more colloquial expression meaning 'my girl'. Oiran were free to reject a customer's advances, but if they assented they would offer a performance of fantasy housewifery, waiting eagerly for their man's return 'home' to the pleasure quarter, dressed in suitable finery – rouged cheeks, black teeth, maybe a cheeky flash of bright green on the lower lip. The *oiran* was dressed for the smartest of dinner parties, albeit in a kimono that carefully afforded a glimpse of crimson inner silks, or even the flesh beneath. Her skin, of course, was painted deathly white – a calculated world away from the natural tawny suntans of the outside, implying a life spent in wealthy, indoor seclusion. The make-up, however, might falter at the neckline, affording the would-be client an erotically charged glimpse of the true skin beneath. It is for this reason that the geisha hairstyle so often was upswept at the back, a flash of neck being as thrilling a frisson to the Edo era as a plunging neckline or a stocking top in today's fashions.

Yūjo, less refined sex workers, could be found in the back alleyways, sitting behind lattice windows waiting for trade. For the cheapest, one didn't even need to go to the pleasure quarter itself, as canny entrepreneurs began operating out of the boats that took customers along the rivers and canals to reach it.

Just as Edo Castle attracted its satellite industries of blacksmiths and carpenters, the Yoshiwara gained its own hangers-on. Broad-brimmed *kasa* rain hats, like wicker-work sombreros, became hot sellers in the neighbourhood regardless of the weather, as they allowed travellers a degree of anonymity. Booze sellers and quacks also did a brisk business, particularly among those clients for whom cruel fate had delayed wealth until old age, thereby requir-ing medicinal aid in the bedroom. As Ōi's famous picture made clear, for those that could not afford the prices in the taverns, simple people-watching was often enough of a draw. Some even played to this spectator crowd, airing their bedding in public in order to demonstrate just how richly appointed their inner quarters were.

The glamour, however, did not endure far beneath the surface. The Yoshiwara was unsurprisingly riddled with venereal disease and hard-luck stories of both prostitutes fallen on hard times and clients bankrupted by their addictions. Since modern political dramas were forbid-den in the theatre, the kabuki stage's stock of 'modern plays' often focused on Yoshiwara tales. For those women who did not live the dream of retiring to start their own establishments, or being bought out of servitude by wealthy clients in search of exclusive mistresses, the end was liable to be ignoble. After death, most sex workers ended up wrapped in a straw mat – the prescribed means for disposing of a pet – and dumped over the wall of the Jōkan-ji temple in what is now Minowa on the Hibiya line. The temple still stands today and claims to host some 25,000 souls, 11,000 of them women of the Yoshiwara.

A century before the advent of television, the theatre

was the big crowd-pleasing medium. There was a classical tradition, Nō, but it was an erudite and rarefied entertainment for the elites. The more vibrant excitement of kabuki came packed with song, dance and scandal, often ripping its stories from the gossip of the day, or thinly disguising representations of real events in order to evade the government censor. Its actors were megastars, the subject of an entire art-print portrait subgenre of performers in their most famous roles, or in rare, offstage repose. Since no women were allowed on the stage (early Shōguns regarded this as tantamount to hookers showing their wares), the female impersonators also became the ultimate mansplainers, giving advice to women about the best way to wear their hair or do their make-up. The plays themselves were boisterous affairs, periodically interrupted by appreciative cries from the audience – theatre managers would plant claques in the crowd to push everyone into having a good time. The actors wore bulky larger-than-life costumes and were adorned with surreal face paint to accentuate their underlying characters, sometimes making their theatrical entrance through the audience on the *hanamichi*, an off-centre catwalk that brought them 'up-close and personal'. With heavy competition from the *bunraku* puppet theatre, whose marionette stars could defy gravity and wow the audience with what we might today call special effects, the kabuki theatre came equipped with special effects of its own, including a spring-loaded trapdoor that allowed for sudden, magical appearances out of nowhere.

Drama has evolved far beyond the cadences and setups that once wowed the residents of old-time Edo, but kabuki itself has not been allowed to evolve along with it. It is frozen in its nineteenth-century heyday as a cultural artefact – a window on a world that used to be. And what a world! Stories from the Japanese theatre formed the bedrock of all Japanese drama that followed, from the melancholy, doomed lovers of *The Love Suicides at Sonezaki*, to the heroics of the medieval hero Yoshitsune in multiple works. Perhaps the most influential was *Yotsuya Kaidan*, a.k.a. the *Tōkaidō Ghost Stories*, based on several urban myths reported around the Yotsuya area in what is now Shinjuku. Eel fishermen told tall tales about a man who found a pair of corpses in his nets – lovers, entwined in a grotesque suicide. Peasants gossiped about an angry husband who killed his wife and her lover, nailing them to opposite sides of a wooden plank and throwing it in the river. Writer Tsuruya Nanboku IV collected the stories and hammered them into a coherent whole. It had its premiere in July 1825 – kabuki horror tales were often staged in the hot summer to give people chills.

It was the most scandalous media event of its day, with rehearsals plagued by arguments, a big-name star determined to rewrite the script and a story ripped from gory urban myths. Even the marketing provoked controversy: a giant kite-shaped billboard depicted a woman's severed head holding the edges of a kimono in its mouth. As for the plot, the down-at-heel samurai Iemon becomes an umbrella maker to support his wife Oiwa and their newborn child. But the 'girl next door' Osode wants Iemon for herself, and convinces Oiwa that a vial of poison is really a medicine to cure postnatal depression. Iemon cannot bear the sight of Oiwa, who is disfigured by the poison, and hounds her into an early grave, claiming that it is her punishment for an alleged infidelity. But when he marries Osode soon after, she throws back her veil to reveal Oiwa's face! A terrified Iemon hacks off the apparition's head, only to discover that he was hallucinating, and that he has just murdered his second wife.

The story of Iemon and Oiwa brings together many popular strands in Japanese storytelling. In TV drama today, you can't throw a rock without hitting a few cheating couples, a stalker saga of fatal attraction, or a couple of samurai vendettas. *Tokaidō Ghost Stories* even incorporates the token disabled character so beloved of modern screenwriters, with a blind servant who dutifully brushes Oiwa's hair, initially unaware that his comb is tearing it out in bloody clumps.

Theatres continue to stage the play today, abridging the original script and skipping to tourist-friendly highlights such as Iemon's haunting by skeletons and the eerie moment when the dead Oiwa calls out to him as he spears eels in a deep, forbidding pool of dark water. You can see the story's spirit living on in every Japanese horror film. As for Oiwa herself, her spirit was supposedly laid to rest in a Tokyo temple (see Gazetteer: Toshima). Actors and theatre producers still drop in to pray before they put on a show.

The Children of Edo

The pleasure quarter was not only about sex and drama. In mixing the otherwise separate cultures of samurai and merchant, it became a great trendsetter. When a young samurai returned to his rural posting from his alternate attendance in Edo, it would be the pleasure quarter's fashions and slang, its food fads and its entertainments, that he most remembered.

By 1720, Edo's population had crept above 1.3 million, making it the largest city in the world, one-third larger than the next contender, Beijing. The city's two halves still seemed to exist in different realities, with the samurai living in relative comfort on the higher ground of the Yamanote, whereas the merchants, artisans and labourers, fully half the city's population, were crammed onto just 16% of the land, in the Low City.

Although the average samurai resident would spend at least every other year in Edo, he would not necessarily add much to the city's local culture. As the Tokugawa peace extended into decades, and then centuries, the samurai became a warrior caste with nobody to battle, practising increasingly outmoded fighting techniques and bickering about the nature of military theory and loyalty. It was the Low City common folk, living their entire lives in sight of Edo Castle, who regarded themselves as the true *Edokko* (children of Edo). The term persists in modern Japanese, much as cockneys regard themselves as the true Londoners, in contrast to transient folk just passing through.

The typical *Edokko* was obsessed with theatre and unobtainable women, lurid potboiler novels and garish woodblock prints. He – for two out of every three Edo residents were still men – also thought of himself as something of a foodie, enthusing about the local delicacies and frankly esoteric differences between types of common fish and seasoning. Such local pride did not travel well outside the city, where the *Edokko* were usually derided as a clueless and even childish underclass, obsessed with low-culture fripperies, loose women and fast food, entirely at the mercy of their shallow emotions and unable to plan for the future. The self-consciously upper-class nobility of Kyōto, still the official capital, regarded the *Edokko* as lice-infested, ill-mannered bumpkins; the business-minded merchant class of Ōsaka thought of them as sex-mad wastrels.

The transient nature of Edo's population – both the samurai on temporary tours of duty and the labourers living hand to mouth – led some unknown wag to refer to it with a Buddhist term: *ukiyo*. Originally meaning 'sorrowful world', a reflection of the guaranteed decline and decay of all material things, this word was co-opted by the children of Edo. They switched one of the kanji characters to spell the word differently, creating a homo-phone of *ukiyo* with a more effervescent meaning. Life was but a dream, they said, so live it! Enjoy it! Thrill at the theatre, have sex at the Yoshiwara. Spend, love, live – for tomorrow there might be a fire or a flood or an earth-quake. Live for today, in this *ukiyo*, this 'floating world'.

Of course, the samurai authorities hated the very idea. In the peacetime environment that the samurai had argu-ably fought to enforce, it was the merchants who were making all the money and having all the fun. While the samurai stoically endured a series of austerity measures, ostensibly to keep them battle-ready and undistracted, edicts warned the merchants not to get ideas above their station, to stop embellishing their possessions with gold leaf or silver filigree. Merchants were scandalously spotted in public dressed like lords and even carrying swords; their women were dressing like princesses, while the average samurai bride struggled to make do.

Most such directives were difficult to enforce. Mer-chants' wives prided themselves on finely wrought treasure chests and classy cosmetics, few of which were seen outside the home. Even architecture started to reflect the merchants' double life – forced to remain in single-storey apartments, they installed secret mezza-nines to expand into the attic space.

'Men take their misfortunes to heart, and keep them there,' observed the writer Ihara Saikaku. 'A gambler does not talk about his losses; the frequenter of brothels, who finds his favourite engaged by another, pretends to be just as well off without her; the professional street-brawler is quiet about the fights he has lost; and a merchant who speculates on goods will conceal the losses he may suffer. All act as one who steps on dog dung in the dark.'

Saikaku (1642–93) was an Edo businessman who turned to writing in his early thirties, seemingly by accident. He found initial success with a thousand-verse poem, composed over a single grief-stricken night after the death of his wife. Abandoning his three children to the care of relatives, Saikaku departed on a quasi-religious pilgrimage, before returning to discover that his poem was a hit. He then launched into a two-decade writing career, aimed at his fellow *Edokko*. His last writings seem to have been an attempt to ingratiate himself with the authorities, chronicling tales of samurai honour and martial achievement, but the bestsellers that made him famous were of an entirely different genre – sensual, erotic tales of the pleasure quarter and everyday sex lives. *Five Women Who Loved Love* and *The Life of an Amorous Man* are perhaps the best known in English. In Japanese, he is more likely to be remembered for *The Life of an Amorous Woman*, which was adapted by Mizoguchi Kenji into the film *Life of Oharu*. Saikaku is perhaps most remarkable today for his egalitarian and matter-of-fact attitude towards homosexuality and pederasty, as seen in his *Great Mirror of Male Love*.

The Magic Hour

The most famous manifestation of the *Edokko* subculture was the *ukiyo-e* (pictures of the floating world), which is to say the thriving industry in woodblock prints that both served and documented the interests of the city dwellers. Beginning around 1700 with monochrome images of famous beauties – pin-ups for *Edokko* bachelors and fashion icons for merchants' wives – the print genre flourished. A ready market was found for printed ephemera that encompassed fantasy epics, tales of derring-do from the distant past and portraits of the celebrities of the floating world – it was asking for trouble to write about or illustrate anything relating to contemporary incidents that might offend the authorities. The industry became adept at self-censorship. The prints were forever being replaced by fresh issues that depicted the latest fashions, current top prostitutes and the season's leading kabuki actors. The books, too, were often loved to death by a series of rental customers, or destroyed in Edo's periodic fires. Despite serious losses of this material over time, enough remains to allow us to assess the scope and style of the floating world.

Among artists of note, of which there are too many to cover in any depth here, Utagawa Kuniyoshi (1798–1861) created a canon of must-see sites in 1833 with his *Famous Views of the Eastern Capital*. While Kyōto, the Emperor's home, retained the stone lantern symbol that denoted it as the true capital, Kuniyoshi's reference to Edo as Tōtō alluded to a growing sense that it was an 'Eastern Capital' only barely subordinate to the imperial city. Kuniyoshi's Edo remains oddly rural in outlook: he focuses on fishermen at work on its many rivers, and views of the city's impressive natural vistas. In one picture, a family of merchants are visiting a temple. The husband is blithely pointing up at a nearby sculpture as if his audience are idiots who cannot see where the big statue is. The child stares up in open-mouthed wonder. The mother's head is turned away from the viewer – her true feelings forever a mystery. It is a charming scene of early tourism, with the statue rendered almost out of focus and more artistic attention given to its visitors – as well as to an oddly Western sense of perspective, and clouds drawn in the sky in a European style. Even though the outside world was supposedly shut out from Japan, elements of it were still creeping in.

Kuniyoshi's glimpses of Edo even extended to the bon viveur. His series *Thirty-Six Fashionable Restaurants of the Eastern Capital* (1852) managed to combine the plots of famous kabuki plays with images of the best-loved performers of the day and images of places to have dinner. For the reader wondering what kind of visual acrobatics are required for such depictions, his *Carpenter Rokusaburō* is a fine example, deriving its subject matter from a play in which the titular labourer chases after two thieves who have stolen a picture of a carp from a restaurant. The fish magically comes to life and struggles with its rescuer, allowing for Kuniyoshi's image to show the actor Onoe Kikugoro II wrestling with a giant fish in the foreground, while the diners of the real-world Yagenori restaurant munch on their seafood platters, oblivious, in the background.

Most famous of all the *ukiyo-e* artists was Katsushika Hokusai (1760–1849), best known abroad for his coloured woodblock print set *Thirty-Six views of Mount Fuji* (which included the iconic *Great Wave Off Kanagawa*) and the 15 volumes of picture references and how-to-draw manuals published in his name, even after his death, which, substantially garbled in transition, eventually gave the world the word *manga*.

Although you will still find woodblock print artists working in Japan today, the industry lacks much of its peak impact and relevance. During the Edo period, woodblock prints were the popular medium of the day and even featured famous actors, who were depicted clutching new cosmetic products in an early form of product placement. The earliest generation of foreign woodblock enthusiasts was understandably interested only in the art. It is only in the twenty-first century, as new scholars emerge with the ability, lost even to most Japanese, to read the spidery background text, that we can start to appreciate the narratives appended to many pictures that often transform their meaning.

Hokusai's infamous *Dream of the Fisherman's Wife*, for

example, once thought to represent a rape, has now been reconceived as a more consensual encounter based on the written dialogue that sprawls across 30% of the image but was ignored by previous foreign critics. Even the title, it turns out, is wrong – its proper name should really be *Diver and Two Octopi*.

Andō Hiroshige (1797–1858) was one of the artists who most lovingly chronicled the Edo of his day and also life on the trunk roads that led into the city. Appealing to the armchair travellers of the times both within the city and out in the provinces, looking forward to a visit or longingly back at one, his late work *One Hundred Famous Views of Edo* offers a glimpse of the last days of the samurai-era city. Kites fly above the Hibiya valley; a barrack-like row of textile dealers' shops is distinguished only by the white lettering on their blue *noren* curtains; a waterfall is frozen in time so completely that it towers above onlookers like a black monolith; walkers on a wooden bridge scurry for cover beneath a sudden downpour. Hiroshige's Edo is an overwhelmingly beautiful city, suffused with greenery and clean-swept streets. It lacks the bustle and implied noise of some of Hokusai's works on similar themes, and is approached with a distinctly modern eye, often captured at the 'magic hour' as sunrise or sunset introduces a softer, more ambient light. His landscapes owe a debt to European prints imported by the Dutch. It is this 'alien' element in his art that often made his landscapes so attractive to Western collectors. Like the classiest of picture postcards, Hiroshige's work captures an idealised and dreamy view of the city – we should never forget that, although they are valuable as historical documents, such pictures were intended to evoke nostalgia for an Edo devoid of poverty and grime that many preferred to remember, even though many of the vistas had already disappeared.

Even the colours are not to be trusted. A century and a half after the pictures were first made, many of them have been hung in the open, beneath light that can cause the subtleties to bleach out. Over time, paints that are produced using animal or vegetable dyes lose their vibrancy, while mineral-based Prussian blue holds its colour, giving the blue in many Japanese prints today an unwarranted dominance. Even when we look at Edo as its residents saw it, we must remember that time has allowed the colours to fade.

4

The Eastern Capital: 1853–1923

His statue is in the corner of Ueno Park, where it has become the default meeting point for anyone heading to the zoo or the area's multiple museums. To say it is a bizarre artistic choice is an understatement. Saigō Takamori (1828–1877) was the legendary 'last samurai', an instrumental figure in the upheavals that heralded the modern era. Pugnacious and stubborn, he was the kind of man you would definitely want on your side in a fight, even if he had a habit of starting a few.

Stocky, with a thick neck supporting a bullet-like head, Saigō looked like the kind of good-hearted strongman who was not quite sure what he was doing when he backed his Satsuma countrymen in overthrowing the Shōgun. His statue marks the site of a victory in the establishment of a new order, although only nine years after the Battle of Ueno he would turn on the new regime in a doomed revolt of his own. Perhaps as a sop to the grumbles of the fading samurai class, perhaps as an attempt to restore the reputation of a man who was, after all, a wayward family member of a faction within the new government, a statue of Saigō was commissioned from Takamura Kōun, who had also worked on the statue of Kusunoki Masashige outside the Imperial Palace. But Saigō was still something of a hot potato – depict him in samurai armour, and he might become a symbol of rightful dissent. Instead, he was shown dressed casually for hunting, a little dog by his side. Or, if you were feeling uncharitable, he appeared like a tramp in a dressing gown leading a mutt on a piece of string. However, nobody was all that sure what Saigō had looked like. He had shunned the modern devilry of photography, and although he was much celebrated in posthumous portraiture, all such images derived from a mash-up drawn by Edoardo Chiossone six years after his death, mixing elements of a brother and a cousin who were said to resemble him.

The statue was unveiled in 1898. Perhaps because this far-right revolutionary has been tempered a little by being shown as a fat-faced man with a dog, he is something of a cherished figure among Tokyo people. I've never heard a bad word said about him, and his statue became not merely a meeting point for lovers and park-goers, but an assembly point in times of trouble. After the firebombing of Tokyo in 1945, the area around his statue was plastered with notices from families who had been separated from their loved ones and feared that they were dead. The statue seemed to have been chosen for this function as a grass-roots noticeboard because it had been used for that purpose once before, in 1923, when Tokyo was shaken to its core and razed to the ground – it was simply the most logical place to meet someone you had lost.

The Black Ships

The rigid class distinctions of the early Edo period had by this time started to erode. As the power of the samurai waned and the merchants rose, they often exchanged places, or at least met in the middle. Some samurai fell on times so hard that they voluntarily gave up their status, freeing themselves to work as merchants. Although there were undoubtedly some success stories, in period slang the term 'warrior business' referred to one whose proprietor was clueless and out of touch, who had dived into commerce as if that were the easy option and discovered all too quickly that it was not.

Others married their children into money, adopting merchant sons-in-law in order to bring samurai status to them, and money back into the family coffers. But all such upheavals pointed to a wider social problem. The samurai had spent two and a half centuries treating the status quo as a mere holiday from an ongoing civil war, without considering the pay-off – that they were an increasingly idle military aristocracy with no incoming spoils, no real way to generate wealth and a habit of pointlessly prizing the technology and values of the sixteenth century.

The Industrial Revolution had transformed the world outside Japan, radically closing distances that might have formerly taken years to cross. For centuries, the Japanese had relied on limited contact with a ghetto of Dutch merchants to keep them informed about the outside world – now the Dutch were warning them that coal-fired ships from other countries risked unsettling the Shōgun's peace.

Japanese waters were tested almost annually by foreign ships attempting to trade with the locals, and there was a profitable smuggling culture in some of the southern domains. But Edo was ill prepared for the American Commodore Matthew Perry and his infamous Black Ships sailing into the bay in July 1853, dropping anchor in spite of pleas not to do so and demanding a meeting with the Shōgun. The United States of America, which had not even existed when the Tokugawa Shōgunate shut out foreigners in the 1630s, now demanded coaling stations and emergency docking facilities for Pacific whalers, as well as the chance to trade with the Japanese. This would be, and still is, remembered as a shocking moment in Japanese history – a bold announcement that the world had changed while the samurai were asleep and that nothing would ever be the same again, starting with the Shōgunate, which was supposed to stop things like this happening.

In the year after Perry's visit, gun emplacements sprang up at the water's edge. Fixed and immobile, they were next to useless in repelling foreign shipping. Indicating just how performative Japanese politics had become, this serious threat was being met not only with outmoded artillery, but with deception. In a common move for Japanese coastal defences of the day, some of the guns were actually fake. Apologists for such trickery regard it as a sign of Japanese smarts at work – considering that such guns were of little real use against enemy attack, the mere sight of them arguably accounted for much of their strategic value. A more cynical historian might suggest that such corner cutting was endemic in much late-Tokugawa military action, and that the last of the samurai were so busy lying to each other about their abilities and technology that they failed to see just how hopelessly outgunned they were in a very real sense. The last vestige of the ill-fated defence strategy endures today on the map of modern Tokyo, where the **Odaiba** ('Gun Batteries') have now been reclaimed and repurposed as an entertainment and convention district.

Anyone of a superstitious mind would find plenty to suggest that disaster was on the horizon. Not long after Perry's visit, Edo was struck by two earthquakes, leading in turn to fires started by overturned cooking stoves, one of which burned down much of the old Yoshiwara. Just to make matters more miserable, a spate of torrential downpours soon flooded much of the Low City and led to an outbreak of cholera. Some turned

superstitious, blaming these misfortunes on the writh-
ing of a giant catfish beneath the city, and fostering a
brief fad for magical charms and talismans to ward off
further disasters. Others turned mean, harping on about
the carpenters and masons who were sure to profit from
other people's misfortunes. The foreigners, however, were
most likely to get the blame, becoming pawns in a power
rivalry between samurai clans that had been dormant for
250 years.

The first sign of trouble came with the suspension of
the *sankin kōtai* system in 1862. Samurai lords were no
longer obliged to spend alternate years in Edo attend-
ing the Shōgun, and they left the city in droves, slashing
the population by up to 300,000. One clan, the Mori of
Nagato, were so keen to put the city behind them that
they actually packed up their mansion and took it with
them, leaving nothing but waste ground.

The samurai went back to their home provinces,
where they brooded and plotted. It was, after all, part of
the Shōgun's job description to be the 'great barbarian-
quelling generalissimo'. If he was unable to keep foreigners
out of Japan, what was he for? The question split the
aristocracy into a web of contending factions – almost
all of them regarding themselves as 'loyalists'. Some were
loyal to the Shōgun and hoped to help him fight off the
foreigners. Others loyal to the Shōgun hoped he would
modernise and learn from the foreigners. Still others
pointed out that the Shōgun was failing in his duty, and
that out of their own sense of loyalty to a higher power,
the Emperor himself, they supported the sacking of the
Shōgun and his replacement by a more qualified candidate, either to throw the foreigners out or accommodate
them – take your pick. Yet more factions pushed their
self-proclaimed loyalty to the Emperor even further,
suggesting that the era of the Shōgun was over, and that

now was the time to restore the Emperor as the head of a constitutional monarchy, all the better for him to either throw the foreigners out or become their friend – once again, depending on how they felt.

This is why the ensuing Japanese civil war is so confusing, with all the above factions plunging into a six-way conflict, firstly with words as they argued over the pros and cons. Matters then turned physical, as the presence of foreigners in Japan proved to be an unbearable affront to young samurai. Nationalist terrorists committed arson attacks and the targeted murders of foreigners and pro-foreign officials, leading to ever-escalating retaliations and concessions from the newcomers. Just who was in charge here? The Shōgun commanded compliance, but then the Emperor commanded him to do his job – an easy thing to say in Kyōto, the residents of which had never stared down the guns of a battleship. The conflict broke out into open war in the 1860s and ended in 1868 with the 'restoration' of the young Emperor Meiji, although neither he nor any of his ancestors for the previous thousand years had been much more than figureheads.

It was not a bloodless coup. Many of the 'battles' of the civil war, it is true, were concluded without a fight, particularly when one canny diplomat, Prince Saionji, developed the habit of unfurling the Emperor's battle flag, daring the so-called loyalists to the Shōgun to charge against it. A song associated with this flag survives as 'nonsense' lyrics in Gilbert and Sullivan's *Mikado*, which accidentally preserves a snatch of real Japanese:

Miya-sama, Miya-sama
On-uma no mae ni
Pira-pira suru no wa
Nan ja na?

The lyrics translate to 'Prince, oh Prince / Before thy horse / What is that which flutters?' The answer – the imperial standard – promised punishment to any rebels who dared defy it. Some rebels, however, still chose to fight. In Tokyo, the bloodiest battle was around the Kan'ei temple in what is now Ueno Park in 1868. Some 2,000 Shōgunal stalwarts made their last stand here, surrounded by imperial forces with modern rifles and Armstrong cannons. Most of the buildings were burned down in the fighting, although the Tōshōgū shrine to Ieyasu himself remained standing. Surveying the smouldering buildings and the 300 corpses of his enemies, so many of them leaking blood that the waters of the Shinobazu Pond turned red, the stocky general Saigō Takamori laughed that his victory was 'an exceptional and extreme delight'.

Leaders of the winning side were ennobled in a new European-style aristocracy, as barons, dukes and viscounts – and even some of the more flexible losers – were incorporated into the new system. The last Shōgun, after his resignation, was swiftly rebranded as a prince. Both his daughter and granddaughter would marry into the imperial family.

If this all sounds confusing, it even confused the samurai themselves. A bunch of them, including the victorious general Saigō, had thought that they were supporting a strong and stable policy of kicking the foreigners out, only to discover that the new order they had helped usher in was intent on rejoining the global economy, welcoming foreigners and foreign technology and scandalously dismantling the samurai system. Modernisation chipped away at everything they held dear; inductees at the new Western-style schools were ridiculed and excluded if they had a samurai haircut. The wearing of swords was forbidden. By the time Saigō realised that he was a turkey voting for Christmas, it was too late. His old feudal domain of Satsuma was abolished, and rezoned as plain old Kagoshima Prefecture. In 1877, he rose up in a doomed revolt against the order he had helped establish. He barely made it out of Kagoshima before he and his most loyal henchmen were surrounded by soldiers with modern artillery. He and his followers had made a last-ditch effort to drag Japan back to the seventeenth century, only to meet with their own deaths.

Some of the Shōgunal loyalists sunk into obscurity. Others scrambled to earn a crust in the new order – ironically meaning that many found themselves working as servants for the only sector of the population that would have them: foreigners. This confronted many a foreign businessman or diplomat with not only the possibility of murderous rebels in his own household, but also the opportunity of a thriving business in newfound antiquities – silk fabrics, swords and lacquerwork sold off on the cheap by former samurai families that had lost everything. The curiosity shops of distant Europe filled up with enough Japanese oddities to spark a whole new art movement, while the stories of samurai daughters falling on hard times and being forced into indentured service and prostitution, told and retold on several occasions, would eventually inspire Puccini's opera *Madama Butterfly* (1904). Butterfly, the 15-year-old girl sold to the US naval officer Pinkerton, arrives with a pitiful collection of knick-knacks that is all that remains of her family's once-great wealth: 'Handkerchiefs, a pipe / A sash, a little clasp / A mirror, a fan' and her proudest possession, the knife that the Emperor presented to her father as an order to commit suicide, engraved with a legend: 'He dies with honour who cannot live without honour.'

Perhaps in recognition that the times were changing, and that the old Japan bore deep scars, the Meiji Emperor founded the Yasukuni ('Appeasing the Country') Shrine in central Tokyo in 1869 (See Gazetteer: Chiyoda). Originally intended as a memorial to the dead on all sides in the Meiji Restoration, its remit gradually expanded during Japan's colonial era as a place to honour fallen soldiers in struggles overseas. Japan's increasing militarisation caused a huge expansion in the number of the war dead, as the nation's soldiery fought wars of conquest against China and then Russia, annexed Korea and advanced into the South Seas.

Edo Becomes Tokyo

The shock of the new soon made itself felt in what had been the Shōgun's city, starting with his castle, which was repurposed as the Imperial Palace – although the Emperor did not move in for many years, living instead in a mansion in Akasaka while renovations continued. Since the Emperor was now resident in the city, Edo was renamed Tōkyōto or Tōkeito (the 'Eastern Capital'). Eventually, this was contracted to just plain Tōkyō. In contemporary English usage, the macrons denoting long vowels tend to be omitted, creating the city's internationally recognised modern name.

By 1869, it had been opened to foreign trade, an act that appeared to please absolutely nobody. The Japanese twitched at yet more concessions to the barbarians, while the barbarians themselves were unimpressed by the city's infrastructure, as E. G. Holtham observed in *Eight Years in Japan*:

> As a commercial port, Tokyo was of no value to foreigners, having no convenient harbour, the nearest roadstead being five miles away, outside the forts of Shinagawa; and though a custom house, bonded

warehouses, etc., had been started at Tsukiji, very
little had been made of them owing to the superior
convenience of Yokohama, less than twenty miles
away.

The 'flowers of Edo' remained a constant threat. 'It
is impossible,' wrote the British diplomat Rutherford
Alcock, 'to ride through the streets... without noticing
one of the most striking and constant features of the city,
no matter what the season of the year – large gaps where
charred timber and rubbish mark the scene of a recent
fire.' It was, thought Alcock, a remarkable night when
one's sleep was not disturbed by the ringing of a fire bell
and the subsequent commotion.

One such fire in 1872 destroyed most of the **Ginza**
('Silver Mint') area, leaving it ripe for development just
as Japan embraced new materials and modes of living. A
whole swathe of modern buildings sprang up, designed
by the Irish civil engineer Thomas Waters, leading to its
nickname of Bricktown, although it was not quite the
hit that investors were hoping for – many Japanese businesses couldn't afford the rents, which were astronomical
even then. Local poets overenthusiastically claimed that
the two-storey structures were towers 'as high as mountains', but foreigners steered clear of streets that looked
just like every other country in the world – they had
come for little temples and quaint pagodas, after all. As
time passed, it became clear that the Ginza Bricktown
buildings were singularly inappropriate for the Tokyo
climate, in which their leaky roofs, poor ventilation and
propensity for dampness encouraged whole colonies of
insects and vermin.

Edward S. Morse, the mollusc authority we first
encountered in Chapter 1, made one of the most compelling remarks about street scenes in 1870s Tokyo, during

his sojourn there as a professor of zoology. 'I had repeatedly observed that young men in the street were never accompanied by girls unless it was a father with his little daughter. The girls are always seen alone, or in company with other girls, or with their mothers.' Asking around his Japanese male colleagues, Morse was astonished to discover that none of them had any female friends. In Tokyo, as in the rest of Japan in the 1870s, it was deemed fitting even for married women to walk a few paces behind their husbands. The concept of the two sexes keeping one another company was private, and the forming of relationships a matter for careful consultation with approved go-betweens. 'With this rigid separation of the sexes socially,' sighed Morse wistfully, 'the boys and girls of Japan lose a great many innocent and happy experiences.'

It is not difficult to imagine the incredible disruption brought to such customs by the onrush of modernity. The traveller Isabella Bird, newly arrived in Tokyo in 1878, wrote to her sister that people were still getting used to the town's new name, and that the former capital, Kyōto, was now supposed to be called Saikyō (the 'West Capital'). Although Saikyō never seems to have stuck, the name Tokyo carried with it enough of a frisson of the new and the modern to catch on. Bird herself observed that 'it would seem like an incongruity' to travel to the samurai city of 'Edo' on a steam train, but journeying in such a fashion to the newfangled Tokyo seemed somehow apt.

The name Tokyo took off rapidly – by the time Bird was writing, it seemed that only foreign tourists used the term Edo. Any Japanese conservative or hidebound enough to adhere to the old samurai-era name was unlikely to be living in the city anymore. Bird does not seem to have realised that even the mode of her travel was a radical transformation – until the Meiji era, the city had favoured foot traffic and canals. The adoption of wheeled traffic – carriages, carts and the train – was a sudden, drastic change to the local way of life. The *jinriki-sha* ('man-powered cart'), swiftly mangled into 'rickshaw', is not mentioned in historical sources before 1869. In a nod to the influence of the Victorian British on customs and laws, Meiji-era traffic began driving on the left – Japan is one of the few countries that continues to follow this custom.

The railway was a typical chimera of the period, built and operated by Europeans, but stocked with staff and clientele from Japan. Bird found it all very strange, sitting practically alone in plush first class while third class was crammed with locals. 'The Japanese look most diminutive in European dress,' she observed. 'Each garment is a misfit and exaggerates the miserable physique and the national defects of concave chests and bow legs.' She had trouble telling how old the officials were; they looked like teenagers to her but turned out to be middle-aged. She also had difficulty identifying the capital itself, detraining at Shinbashi to find herself asking passers-by where 'Tokyo' was. The city, she reported, 'has no smoke and no long chimneys; its temples and buildings are seldom lofty; the former are often concealed among thick trees, and its ordinary houses seldom reach a height of 20 feet.' In the distance, she saw a vivid blue sea, dotted with fortified islands and scattered with fishing boats. Closer at hand were the Japanese themselves. 'I feel as if I had seen them all before,' she wrote, 'so like are they to their pictures on trays, fans, and tea-pots.'

As Bird travelled through the streets to the British legation, she looked out on a sight that she found drab and uninspiring, although to the historian it is a breathtaking glimpse of the last remnants of the Tokugawa era:

I cannot tell you anything of what I saw on my way thither, except that there were miles of dark, silent, barrack-like buildings, with highly ornamental gateways, and long rows of projecting windows with screens made of reeds – the feudal mansions of Yedo.

The samurai mansions near the Imperial Palace no longer served any purpose. Once they had housed loyal nobles on their attendance to the Shōgun, but with the Shōgun gone, the real estate had other uses, and was earmarked for government offices. The new Ministry of Finance was constructed on the site of the old Sakai mansion in Ōtemachi – deriving its name from Ōtemon, the main gate to Edo Castle, of which only the foundation stones now remain. The grounds of the ministry retained the lily pond of the old mansion gardens, along with the imposing mound of Kubizuka, legendarily believed to be the resting place of the head of Masakado. Only one element remained unchanged from earlier times – the stone stele that somehow bound Masakado's restless spirit to keep the peace had been removed.

Ominous black birds seemed to bring Masakado's spirit to the air, as the missionary doctor Henry Faulds wrote:

> The cleansing of the streets is greatly assisted by armies of large, raven-beaked crows (*Corvus japonensis*) and rather kingly-looking black-eared kites (*Milvus melanotis*) which may be seen in myriads, on a calm day, circling at a great height above the city. They have a curious guttural, tremulous cry...

More than a century since, this does not seem to have changed a whole lot – Tokyo's crows remain a constant presence in the city, and their cries are a feature of any Tokyo moment that is otherwise quiet.

The area around the Kanda Left Gate, former home to many a *daimyō*, was already falling into disrepair by the time of the Restoration – it was deemed too close to the bustle of the city, and most of the richer residents had already moved out. A fire in 1869 destroyed most of the buildings and presented the city with a clean slate. Determined to ward off future blazes, officials constructed the Akiba Jinja (Autumn Leaf Shrine) amid the ruins, leading to the area's new name of **Akihabara** ('Plain of Autumn Leaves'). The shrine was moved in 1888 when the local train station was built, but the name stuck. Soon an important junction for freight trains, the Akihabara region became known as the location of a vibrant and occasionally suspect market, where traders dealt in fresh vegetables, some of which may have been lifted from the rail yards.

Sometimes, the city appeared to participate in its own destruction. A fierce flood in 1885 dislodged the Senju Bridge and sent it barrelling down the Sumida River, where it smashed into and demolished the famous Azuma Bridge to Akasaka. The Azuma crossing got an ultra-modern steel replacement in 1887, which was eventually reinforced to allow trams to use it.

One suspects that sometimes these crises were welcomed at the city planning office, where government policymakers were keen to reinforce Japan's imperial ambitions by making Tokyo 'the greatest city in Asia' and in the words of one minister for home affairs 'the model for all cities in the empire'. An entire generation of civil servants had now been trained abroad and was determined to turn Tokyo into a new London or Paris, fit to impress foreign visitors with the speed of Japan's transformation. It needed to become a city suitable for its now-resident Emperor, with economic and political importance to match. The diarist Kumi Kunitake, returning in 1872 from a fact-finding mission abroad, told his bosses what needed to be done by observing what had made the greatest impact on him in Europe:

> Across the length and breadth of London we did not see a single unpaved street. In Paris, around the Arc de Triomphe, broken stone is laid tightly, and gravel is spread on top. When you enter any country [for the first time], you can tell immediately, by looking at the road surfaces, whether the government is efficient or not and whether the citizens are likely to be rich or poor.

Paris, Kume noted, had been a dingy, medieval city of small streets until it had been transformed by the political ambitions of Napoleon III. Tokyo should do the same. The changes in land usage created fluctuations in district prices. Marunouchi, the outer area of the castle, was no longer required for barracking soldiers – Japan was protected by a modern army – suddenly creating a derelict, deserted area ringing the Emperor's home. Nobody seemed to have a good plan for its conversion – what *do* you do with land in sight of a living god? Eventually, the land was sold to Iwasaki Yanosuke from the family that owned Mitsubishi, a company that had reached new heights by providing much of the logistics, provisions and equipment for the ever-growing modern army. Iwasaki started pouring money into the area, intent on creating a truly modern business district – beginning with Mitsubishi's new corporate headquarters, the centrepiece of the 'London Block', named after its deliberate resemblance to the architecture of the British capital. Iwasaki hired a London-born architect, Josiah Conder (1852–1920), to design it. Only 27 at the time of his arrival in Japan, Conder juggled the teaching of his discipline with its practice, effectively training up the generation of Japanese that would eventually supplant him and make him honorary president of the Architectural Institute of Japan. He might have started the London Block, but its crowning achievement came a generation later, when one of his students designed the Victorian red-brick temple that was the Tokyo railway station in its midst. The station elegantly symbolised an imperial space in the heart of an imperial city, and finally brought bustle to a district that had been so slow to develop that local wags had previously christened it the *Mitsubishi-ga-hara* (Mitsubishi wastelands).

While he taught the men who would replace him, Conder was the chief architect for the frankly European look of the brick-built buildings that sprang up around the Imperial Palace: university faculties, ministry offices, churches and eventually Iwasaki's mansion and even his mausoleum. He is best remembered for the Rokumei-kan (the 'Hall of the Crying Deer'), a palace in a French Renaissance style, completed in 1883 and intended to both make foreign dignitaries feel at home, and also convey the message of just how modern Japan had become. Pierre Loti, the French author of *Madame Chrysanthème*, dismissed the whole thing with a Gallic shrug, sneering that it looked like a second-rate casino, and that the attempts of the Japanese to conduct themselves at a European-style ball were about as convincing as a 'monkey show'.

Needless to say, this is not how the Rokumeikan was received by the Japanese themselves. It became popular with progressives as a symbol of Japan's embrace of the West, and with conservatives as a sign of the decline in standards brought about by such pandering. It was the most famous building in Tokyo for a few glorious years in the 1880s, before the opening of the nearby Imperial Hotel in 1890 rendered its original purpose redundant, and it was repurposed as a gentlemen's club. It endured until 1941, when its demolition in wartime Japan was regarded as a comment on the rejection of Western values.

The Banishment of Shadows

The technology gap between samurai-era Japan and the modern world meant that a number of developments were dropped into the Japanese world so fast that they gave observers whiplash. Coal-fired factories belched smoke into the air, combining with the swampy atmosphere of the canals and the Low City to create, in the words of the British Japanologist Basil Hall Chamberlain, 'that damnable mixture of muck, mildew and miasma, which at Tokyo masquerades under the name of air'.

Chamberlain, who still is famed as an orientalist, was entertainingly vicious about how much he hated Tokyo, which he regarded as a ghastly slum with ideas above its station, where even the ex-pats were horrible people. But his protests were soon drowned out by visitors who found the city to be far more beguiling, such as the writer Douglas Sladen, whose questionably titled *The Japs at Home* compared Tokyo to both Rome and Venice, calling it 'one of the most delightful cities I was ever in. It is wonderfully beautiful, so undulating, so full of magnificent temples and groves, so full of Japanese land and water life'. The 'water life', however, was receding, as the din of the modern world began to encroach on the city denizens, causing the rapid decline of Tokyo as a canal city in favour of the clatter of cartwheels on stone streets, and the clang of hammers in new industries. In some cases, this caught businessmen by surprise: one of old Edo's best restaurants had been located to catch river traffic, and suddenly found itself too far from the main thoroughfare.

Henry Faulds was glad to see the canals go, since he regarded them as death traps:

> The canals near us were usually lively in the hot days with schoolboys bathing, and frequently there would be a shout and a sudden rush of people; an hour or so afterwards a pale little limp and lifeless corpse would be dragged out, still clutching firmly a tuft of *chara* or some other water-weed, under the cruel coils of which the swiftly out-rushing tide had dragged the poor child. Often with sore heart I tried to get something done to prevent those pitiful accidents, as people called them, but almost in vain.

There was no gradual procession of street lighting from occasional gas lamps to electricity. Instead, Tokyo found itself lit up within a single generation. Writers of the electrification period mourned the banishment of shadows, claiming that the ghosts and spirits that had once riddled every corner of Tokyo's streets were fleeing ever further into the dark countryside. The stars overhead, once a common topic in poetry and song, became increasingly harder to pick out, and the romance and danger of wandering a lonely night-time pathway, lantern in hand, became a thing of the past. Late nights themselves became part of social life – the opening ball at the Rokumeikan finished long past the bedtime of the average Tokyo resident, who was used to rising at dawn and heading home at sunset.

Electric light also affected the indoor life of Tokyo's inhabitants. Working days that had once ended with the dusk could now be extended for evening appointments. Perhaps the most noticeable effect was that on kabuki. Our sense today of what constitutes a kabuki performance is somewhat ruined by our ability to see every corner of the well-lit stage. Actors once crept around in shadows, illuminated by candles held aloft by invisible attendants. Traditional Tokugawa-era kabuki held the attention of its audiences by focusing on single moments and faces. The stagehands, meanwhile, were entirely invisible. Clad head to foot in black, they slipped easily into shadows, making the special effects of levitation, transformation and disappearance all the more thrilling. Today, the 'invisible' attendants could not be more visible if they were painted pink and wearing clown shoes, removing much of the original drama and excitement.

The old guard were similarly wary of telegraph lines, which soon criss-crossed the city, creating perches for birds and the unsightly image of the sky tied up with wires. The pastime of flying kites, which were once a regular sight in the skies, was banned as a health hazard. In a precursor of the 'tinfoil hat' brigade of modern times, some entrepreneur came up with a design for a thin metal fan allowing the doubting samurai to shield his brain from electric waves every time he passed beneath one of the wires. But sometimes there was no way to resist the effects of modernisation. Portraits of the era's trendsetters often show that it was now necessary to brandish a pocket watch; the increasing noise of the modern city had drowned out the tolling of the temple bells that traditionally marked the time.

The old ways were dying out, but many of their proponents were determined to go out with a bang. As photography took over in magazines and on walls, the last of the woodblock print artists struggled to adapt to the changing world. Tsukioka Yoshitoshi (1839–92) was highly representative of the era: whereas the old aristocracy was fading, Yoshitoshi was the son of a merchant who had bought his way into samurai status. An apprentice and possibly nurse to the ageing artist Utagawa

Kuniyoshi, Yoshitoshi established a name for himself in the early Meiji era with his grotesque, violent and often disturbing 'bloody prints'. His images of murders, suicides and rapes, suffused with bondage and gore, presented a literally visceral alternative to the heroic prints of other artists. Today, these works have an off-the-wall following, although they are representative of neither Yoshitoshi's overall body of work, nor what Japanese audiences found desirable. By the 1870s, he was reduced to poverty and depression, but found a new outlet drawing reportage and true-crime images for the growing periodical market. His work saw a final flourishing of *ukiyo-e*, particularly in his much-praised *One Hundred Aspects of the Moon*, the nocturnal nature of which presented a challenge to any artist, but which came alive in his hands both in art and poetry. 'Holding back the night,' Yoshitoshi wrote, 'with increasing brilliance / the summer moon.'

Times remained hard – he managed to persuade two of his girlfriends to sell themselves to brothels to help support him – but he ended his life as one of the champions of woodblock prints. One of his pupils, Migita Toshihide, would truly be among the last *ukiyo-e* print-makers, producing some startling images of modern times at the turn of the twentieth century, before woodblock art suffered a change in priorities – it ceased to strive to represent Japan as it really was, and began depicting Japan as the more beautified setting that foreign visitors wished it to be. Pushed out of reportage and popular publishing by the rise of photography, woodblock art became an artistic treasure, but was no longer a 'popular' medium.

By the time Rudyard Kipling visited Tokyo in 1889, the foreign love-in was in full swing:

Here you saw how Western civilisation had eaten into them. Every tenth man was attired in Europe

clothes from hat to boots. It is a queer race. It can
parody every type of humanity to be met in a large
English town. Fat and prosperous merchant with
mutton-chop whiskers; mild-eyed, long-haired
professor of science, his clothes baggy about him;
schoolboy in Eton jacket.... But when you come
to speak to the imitation, behold it can only talk
Japanese.

Like some baffled Victorian Mr Bean, Kipling blundered
down the street, addressing 'the most English-looking
folk [he] saw'. Much to his surprise, although presumably
not to anyone else's, nobody he ran into understood him.

The Westernisation of Tokyo continued without
waiting for Kipling's approval. In 1900, the poet Masaoka
Shiki summed up the speed of development with a poem
that symbolised the crash of modernity into tradition:

Glimpsed in luminous moonlight
The woods of Ueno—
Then my home shaken and rattled
By passing locomotives

Tokyo's footprint tripled overnight in 1893, when
the land around the upper reaches of the Tama River, a
major source of water supply and building lumber, was
handed back to the city's authority (Tokyo having lost
this area when the boundary was redrawn in 1871). In
1880, the city gained its weirdest and farthest outposts:
the Ogasawara Islands in the Pacific Ocean, a thousand
kilometres to the south. In 1891, these islands were aug-
mented with the addition to Tokyo's administrative area
of a small scattering of volcanic outcrops even further
away, including Iwo Jima. The incorporation of all these
islands into 'Tokyo' was in part an accident of boundaries

and administration, but also plainly calculated to shoo away other colonial powers. The islands had been 'discovered' on multiple occasions, in 1543 by the Spanish and in 1670 by the Japanese, who retroactively named them for Ogasawara Sadayori, a samurai who claimed to have found them in 1593. In 1827 they were claimed by the British, leading to a small settlement of Anglo-Hawaiian colonists who were granted Japanese citizenship after the 1891 takeover. Prehistoric relics on the islands suggest that they had in fact been discovered thousands of years earlier by proto-Japanese, but had then been forgotten.

In 1903, Tokyo got its first European-style park in Hibiya, open all hours and soon thereby attracting scattered pairs of canoodling couples. The old troop barracks were moved out to Aoyama, and the area was landscaped with fountains and trees. Technology played a part too, with Tokyo's electric tram network coming online that same year, making it possible for large groups of visitors to convene in a single place at short notice. This chance confluence of technology and urban design led to Hibiya Park's unplanned role as a place for protests and political rallies, beginning in 1905 after the government, nearly bankrupted by the Russo–Japanese War, signed a treaty that handed back some of the spoils. A crowd of 30,000 descended on Hibiya Park, pushed through the police barricades, spilled out into the city in an angry procession and eventually ran amok, setting fire to institutions somehow blamed for the 'betrayal' of the negotiated peace settlement (a newspaper, a politician's house). The riot ultimately caused 17 deaths and many more injuries. The authorities proclaimed several days of martial law. It was not quite the 'park life' they had imagined.

The Cloud-Surpassing Tower

For a good century, from just before the coming of the Black Ships to the city's destruction and rapid remodelling in the 1940s, the centre of Tokyo life was the Asakusa district. This is somewhat ironic, since it owes its very existence to attempts by the authorities to stop it being the centre of *anything*. Asakusa had become the new home of the kabuki theatres in 1841, after disapproving officials ordered them banished from the city centre. And so, the new entertainment district was set up at a location that was then outside the city, albeit handy for the river boats on the Sumida, and at the foot of the Azuma Bridge. Much to the authorities' annoyance, customers were soon making the effort to visit. Two hours' walk from the city gate had seemed like a long way in 1841, but within a generation Tokyo had better roads and rickshaw runners, horse-drawn carriages and trams. The city grew out to meet Asakusa.

Asakusa was the place to see kabuki theatre and attendant sideshows, magic lanterns and, as modernisation rushed onward, Tokyo's first dedicated cinemas. Its temples presented the ideal excuse for the young to head into town either for prayers, fairs and festivals – chance or not-so-chance encounters for courting couples, and prostitutes offering a rental experience. The streets of Asakusa thrummed with restaurants and cafés. It became the place to try newfangled foods like the *ushinabe* stew that broke with Buddhist tradition by containing beef, a popular fad with former soldiers from the civil war, some of whom had been encouraged to try it in hospital to keep their strength up. The philosopher Fukuzawa Yukichi was scandalised by it. He observed, 'We had no idea where the meat came from, whether it was slaughtered or died of disease. It was very cheap, so we could fill up with beef and sake and rice, but the beef was very tough and smelly.' Some still preferred to take the meat in the more traditional 'medicinal' fashion and settled for a 'cow bowl' of rice with a few beef scraps experimentally scattered on top (see Eating and Drinking). It was the place for grazing on street food and sampling new teas and imported coffees.

The railway line reached the area in 1902, and by 1910 the station at Azuma Bridge had been renamed Asakusa in an attempt to associate it with the neighbourhood. At its heart stood the greatest marvel of all, the Ryōunkaku ('Cloud-Surpassing Tower'). It was designed by the Scotsman William Kinnimond Burton (1856–1899), a self-taught jack-of-all-trades who had come to Japan as a sanitation engineer but whose legacy today lives on through the many valuable photographs he took. Despite having only a draughtsman's experience that ran to sewage works and water filtration parks, Burton somehow found himself designing the centrepiece of the entertainment quarter. He came up with the Ryōunkaku, which was completed in 1890 and is regarded as Tokyo's first sky-scraper. This 12-storey octagonal tower offered what was then the best view of Tokyo, from the observation galleries on its top three floors. On a clear morning, you could still see all the way to Mount Fuji. On New Year's Day in 1891, the new tower was publicised by the release from its top floor of a set of balloons, each bearing a visitor's ticket. The fight on the ground for these prized items was so fierce that only one ticket stayed intact enough to be cashed in.

On the ninth floor was an art gallery, and on the eighth a lounge, reachable from the ground, at least at first, by two electric elevators. These contraptions were installed by Fujioka Ichisuke, a light-bulb seller whose company would eventually become one of the founding pillars of Toshiba. The elevators, however, only served for six months before they were shut down because of 'safety concerns', but however visitors made it to the observation deck, they would have to exit via the gift shops on the seven lower floors. Forty-six stores sold exotica from all around the world, giving even the humblest of Tokyo locals a chance to sample wares from far-flung Europe, Africa and America.

The Cloud-Surpassing Tower was a beacon of modernity, its lower floors obscured by a massive billboard for Jintan breath mints, its upper floors the inevitable target of Tokyo residents in search of a one-stop day out, where they could take in the view, visit an art gallery, drink something horrible from a foreign country, try some weird food and buy some knick-knacks. Locals were ridiculously proud of it, and usually referred to it as Asakusa Jūni-kai ('Asakusa Twelve Floors') just to rub in its location and height.

It stood, however, for only 33 years before it came crashing down. Tremors in 1894 weakened the structure, leading to the buttressing of Burton's red-brick walls with steel girders – but the tower, along with much of the rest of Tokyo, was damaged beyond repair in 1923, when the city was struck by a cataclysmic earthquake.

The disaster's correct full name is the Great Kantō Earthquake, as it affected much of the Kantō Plain. The epicentre was on the outskirts of Yokohama, which suffered as much as, if not worse than, Tokyo itself. The initial damage, of course, came from collapsing buildings, but the quake struck just before lunchtime on a windy day, inevitably starting hundreds of small fires from upended cooking stoves, which rolled up into a city-wide firestorm. The Low City, in particular, survived the shaking of the ground, but was then annihilated by the fire, which burned it down in two days. For many, it was a disastrous first encounter with the brittle, heavy consequences of building high structures in brick instead of wood – brick buildings being fire resistant but far more dangerous when they fell down. Other modern technologies proved similarly disastrous – some people fleeing the firestorm found themselves glued to half-melted tarmac until the flames caught up with them. Others sought refuge in the canals and rivers, only for the flames to seep after them on rafts of burning oil. The city burned for two days, creating a pall of black smoke and an unceasing rain of ash.

It would take a decade to recover. In the interim, the heart was cut out of Japan, and those who had the chance relocated south to Ōsaka, or elsewhere in the country. The parks turned into shanty towns, the ruins into building sites. Tokyo was about to transform once more.

5

Tokyo at War: 1923–1952

THE DOG'S STATUE waits patiently outside Shibuya station, his ears alert as if listening for the train, his paws placed firmly on the ground in front of him, in anticipation. His tail has flopped, listless, on the ground, because he has been waiting a long time. These days, he is usually surrounded by a crowd of tourists and selfie takers. Some paw enthusiastically at the bronze hound; others are simply lurking nearby, having unwisely agreed upon the landmark as a meeting spot and forgotten the crowds it always attracts. Hachikō is a dull brown colour, although his forelegs have been rubbed golden-smooth and shiny by millions of well-wishers. When he was alive, from 1923–1935, his fur was a brilliant white.

Hachikō was an Akita puppy when he was acquired by Ueno Hidesaburō (1872–1925), a professor of agriculture at Tokyo Imperial University. The young dog would accompany his master to the station every day and come to meet him at the station in the evening. A year later, in 1925, the 53-year-old Ueno collapsed while giving a lecture, and died at the university. However, Hachikō continued to wait for him each evening at the station, becoming something of a local celebrity, and accorded greater fame by Japan's burgeoning mass media. In 1934, the dog was present at the unveiling of a statue in his honour – seen by old and young as an embodiment of unconditional love and loyalty.

Hachikō died in 1935. His ashes were interred beside his master's in Aoyama Cemetery, although his pelt was mounted and stuffed, and can still be seen in Japan's National Science Museum. The original statue, however, did not outlast him for very long. Hachikō's fame might be viewed today through a prism of sentimentality, but he served a different purpose in his own era, when a Japan newly entrenched in a prolonged war of colonisation and conquest hoped to instil a sense of lifelong, dog-like devotion in its citizenry. That same country-wide co-option into an increasingly hard-fought war effort saw the original statue melted down in the 1940s. A replacement was erected on the same spot in 1948 and can still be found there to this day. It has become such a fixture of Tokyo life that the nearby exit from the station is simply known as Hachikō. On 8 March every year, on the anniversary of his death, there is a solemn ceremony in honour of dogs and their owners. Hachikō has remained a common touchstone in Japanese popular culture, the subject of multiple children's books and movies, and of several additional statues. The most recent statue, and the most touching, was raised on the grounds of Tokyo University itself in 2015 and shows Hachikō leaping on his hind legs with joy as Ueno Hidesaburō returns to greet him at last.

Everybody knows about Hachikō, although even during his lifetime there were those who questioned the truth of his story. It has been suggested that, far from waiting faithfully for his master, he had been practically disowned by the Ueno family and had taken to lurking around the station all day begging for food. Hachikō remains a Tokyo icon, although many are hard-pressed to volunteer much information about his owner. But Ueno Hidesaburō also played a vital role in the history of

Tokyo. As an agricultural engineer, Ueno was a special-ist in land reclamation and drainage; his expertise served him well after the Kantō Earthquake, when he advised on the best way to reconstruct the broken city. He, like many of his countrymen, had originally moved out to Shibuya while the long job of clearing and rebuilding the ruins to the east went on.

After the Quake

One of the many buildings destroyed outright was the Ministry of Finance in Ōtemachi. The entire site was bulldozed, along with the dilapidated remains of a grave mound in the gardens, the stone inner chamber of which was found to be empty. In a flurry of renewal and rebuild-ing, the developers decided to dig the mound out, backfill a nearby pond with earth, level the whole area and put up a prefabricated office so the ministry could keep running. The building, however, soon gained a reputation for being cursed, as it was plagued with accidents, falls and mishaps that claimed 14 lives over the next year, including that of the finance minister himself. By 1928, officials had had enough. The prefabricated building was torn down, the grave mound rebuilt and a Buddhist priest brought in from the nearby temple to hold a 'pacification' rite to expel the spirit of Masakado.

The Imperial Hotel, which had been playing host to foreign bigwigs since the 1890s, burned down in 1922 – shortly after work had started nearby on its namesake, designed by the famous architect Frank Lloyd Wright. This Mayan Revival building was a marvel in poured concrete, and was impressively little damaged by the 1923 Great Earthquake that flattened the rest of the city. 'Hotel stands undamaged as monument to your genius,' an appreciative aristocrat telegrammed after the site was briefly repurposed as housing for those left homeless by the disaster. This, at least, was the official story – in fact, Wright's building had suffered some damage of its own, and was by no means the only pre-quake structure to remain standing in the city.

The Azuma Bridge, which had been through numerous forms since it was first built in 1774, suffered fire damage during the quake and was replaced by an all-iron construction in 1931. Several railway stations nearby, run by rival companies, were now claiming to be 'Asakusa', leading Asakusa station, the former Azumabashi ('Azuma Bridge') station, to be renamed yet again. As the railway networks of Tokyo became ever more intricate, it became incumbent on the names of stations to be more precisely linked to their locations – it was no longer enough to be merely within sight of a particular landmark. The former Azumabashi, and later Asakusa, station was renamed for a smaller canal bridge that was closer – it was now Narihirabashi.

The proliferation of Asakusa stations, however, was a clue that Asakusa was becoming ever more popular, serving an ever-growing number of modern boys and girls out on the town. It had a whole verse to itself in the *Tokyo March*, a song that featured prominently in the 1929 film of the same name by Mizoguchi Kenji, in which a girl sings of the excitements of the city:

Tokyo is wide, but love can be narrow
A secret meeting in stylish Asakusa
You on the subway, me on the bus
Heading for the stop of love.

Shall we see a cinema or take tea?
Or run off together on the Odakyū?
Transforming Shinjuku, that moon of Musashino
Rising over the department stores.

Peppered with neologisms like *jazz* and *rush hour* – some of them used ham-fistedly, as in her desire to 'see a cinema' – the song is thrilled by everything modern, including attitudes. The Odakyū was a railway that could take the couple all the way to the mountains. It, like the phrase 'run off together', is hence tantalisingly ambiguous – is she proposing a little trip, or actually eloping? The idea is jammed in there, and then swiftly overrun with the poetic image of the moon above the shopping arcades, but there it is – she put it out there, a joke-not-joke, a nervous suggestion.

At the time, the real dilemma was over the use of the term Odakyū, to which the stuffy managers of the railway, which was more correctly named Odawara Kyūkō Denki Kidō Kabushiki Kaisha, strongly objected. They demanded that the full name (meaning Odawara Express Electric Transport Company Limited) be used in all song lyrics or not at all. People ignored this absurd imposition and the slangy Odakyū caught on, becoming one of the first of many such contractions in Tokyo transport, reducing many lines and areas to the same type of snappy two-character name that characterised Tokyo itself.

Other changes to the city were only obvious at the local level. The fish market, which had been stinking up Nihonbashi for decades, was finally out of sight and smell in Tsukiji, the former marshland area that had formerly been a foreigners' ghetto. Meanwhile, although people continued to remove their shoes in private homes, in the newer larger-scale public places customers were no longer expected to don slippers just to enter a shop. Occupants of newly built homes attempted to insure themselves against a repeat of the earthquake disaster by replacing open stoves with gas cookers. Faucets and sinks were installed in kitchens, reducing reliance on standpipes, and many of the new ultra-modern houses even included iceboxes.

The post-quake rebuilding of Tokyo would have been the perfect time to sort out its outlandish and idiosyncratic address system, but nobody seems to have bothered. As a result, the former system of house numbering, dating back to the days of feudal block-barracks, remained in place, imparting a ridiculous degree of confusion to later generations. In very rare cases, a corporation would own an entire plot of land, build a single kind of dwelling on it, like a block of flats, and number the living quarters rationally and consecutively. This, however, was not the norm, with house numbers in Tokyo liable to relate not to one's location in a street, but the time at which one's house was built. This confusing system, and the traditional means of navigating it, both echo the old samurai era. Wander into an unfamiliar neighbourhood in search of a friend's house, and in the days before mobile phones, you were liable to be entirely at a loss. There would, inevitably, be a police box, the drowsy denizen of which would be on speaking terms with everybody in the neighbourhood, and would at the very least have a map of the nearest couple of blocks, with every house identified by its owner's surname.

None of this, of course, would have been much of a problem in the samurai era, when everybody knew each other, and when entire city blocks were taken up by enclosures belonging to particular clans. Even in the twentieth century, it was only a problem to outsiders – everybody on the street would know which house was Mrs Matsuda's, and where the plumber lived. The postman was not an anonymous minion but a local character that, by necessity, had to know who everybody was. The policeman in his sentry box did not speed through at 30 miles per hour in a squad car, but pounded the pavements on foot every day, getting to know the locals. Japanese media still periodically harken back to such practices as part of 'the good old days', before neighbours failed to learn each other's names, and when children played in streets that rarely saw an automobile. Today, such a situation appears to be a thing of the past, but the inclusion of maps or directional hints remains a common feature of Japanese business cards, just to spare one's taxi driver the embarrassment of having no idea where to take you. In the twenty-first century, it is at least possible to paste Japanese addresses, many of which look like quadratic equations, straight into Google Maps – a luxury not available to earlier generations of Tokyo city wanderers.

X Marks the Spot

Tokyo's pre-war high point came in 1936, when the city won the bid to host the 1940 Olympic Games, timed to fall on the 2,600th anniversary of the legendary founding of Japan by its first divine Emperor, Jinmu. The victory was a triumph of Japan's relentlessly modernising government, the post-quake clear-up initiatives and the International Olympic Committee itself, which could finally live up to its claim that the games were truly universal. But Japan's militarist government had already initiated an era characterised by constant overseas warfare, having invaded China in 1931. The rhetoric of the Second World War in the West does not usually invoke Japan until the bombing of Pearl Harbor in 1941, but that view ignores the preceding decade of fighting in China that transformed life on the Japanese home front and militarised many aspects of Tokyo life. The clues that the Olympics were a doomed venture were there as early as 1938, when Tokyo backed out of hosting the event because so much steel was being used for the China conflict that there wasn't enough to build a stadium. The venue was switched to Helsinki, and then the Olympics were cancelled anyway because of the war in Europe.

A ban on fun took hold, starting in 1939 when the sale of alcohol was forbidden on Mondays as a reminder of the hardships faced by Japanese soldiers overseas, imparting 1940s Tokyo with a serious austerity. It was unseemly to enjoy oneself too much when soldiers were out on the front line. The coffee shops and cafés shut down or worked on reduced hours, which turned out to be a handy way of avoiding the unpleasant truth: shortages were soon biting so hard they had little left to sell to their dwindling customers. Wrought-iron railings and bronze statues like that of Hachikō – many of the keynote adornments of the Meiji and Taishō eras – were ripped up and melted down for the war effort.

Japanese leaders had been warned, by no less a figure than the 'reluctant admiral', Yamamoto Isoroku, that any victories in the Pacific would be short-lived. Unless Japan perpetually scored a rolling series of impossible wins across the Pacific, onto the West Coast of the US and then across America into the very garden of the White House itself, there would be retaliation – and it would be directed against them with all the might of American industry. His pleas fell on deaf ears. Worse, in fact, they were often misquoted and redacted to make him sound far more gung-ho than he was.

Even the weather had it in for Tokyo. In 1940, a ministry building in Ōtemachi was struck by lightning, creating a swiftly spreading fire that tore through the government district. Nine offices were destroyed, including the Ministry of Finance, causing officials to once more call in a priest to make sure that the angry spirit of local deity Masakado was properly confined in his grave mound. They also ensured that, somewhat belatedly, the stone stele proclaiming a peaceful Buddhist afterlife name for Masakado was restored to the site, a thousand years after Masakado's disembodied head had supposedly flown there.

Tokyo's first clue as to the dragon its leaders had awoken overseas came on 18 April 1942 when 16 American bombers appeared out of nowhere and dropped their loads over the city. These were the Doolittle Raiders, which had taken off on a one-way trip from aircraft carriers to which it would be impossible to return, chancing their luck by flying without fighter escort and hoping to make it with the last of their fuel to crash landings and rescue on the Chinese mainland. It was the first intimation for the Japanese on the ground that the war was not progressing quite as well the news broadcasts were telling them. The population had been assured of continued victories, although it didn't take a genius to see that these 'victories' were being reported closer and closer to the home islands. Owing to an accident of political zoning, the distant Ogasawara Islands, stretching a thousand miles away from Japan, were officially part of the Tokyo metropolis. On 19 February 1945, the United States Marine Corps stormed the island of Iwo Jima – which was, at least on paper, the outskirts of Tokyo itself – in a battle that ended with the Americans raising their flag and acquiring a new airfield in bombing range of Tokyo proper.

The relentless onslaught from the air continued, reaching its most terrible peak in Operation Meetinghouse, a single raid on 9 March 1945 that claimed more than 100,000 lives and left another million homeless. The first wave of B29 Superfortress planes dropped a chain of napalm cluster bombs in an X shape that spanned the city. Subsequent squadrons just dumped their incendiaries somewhere near this fiery target marker, the clear lines of the cross already blurring as fires spread in all directions. The Tokyo air raid was a huge military success, wiping out the small cottage industries that supplied piecework to the larger factories. Such workshops, of course, were based in and around residential homes. More people died in Tokyo that night than would be killed in Hiroshima on the day of the atomic bomb. Entire districts were razed, particularly in the east of the city, which still comprised wood-built houses, along with the flammable lumber yards that had been relocated there after the Meireki Fire of 1657. Soldiers began shooting stray dogs in Hibiya Park, in an attempt to keep them from scavenging the piles of corpses left there for disposal.

A pilot, Raymond Halloran, bailed out from his critically damaged B29 and fell more than 7,000 metres before deploying his parachute. As he swung above the burning city, a Japanese fighter swept past, its pilot saluting him. Captured on landing, Halloran was kept in solitary confinement in 'a cold, dark cage' for 67 days, before being exhibited in Ueno Zoo as 'the hated B29 pilot', covered in insect bites and crawling with lice. There were not a lot of other attractions, the rest of the zoo animals having been poisoned or starved.

It all came to an end in 1945, with Japan reduced to famine levels by bombing campaigns targeted on the sea routes. Some of the leaders of the armed forces were determined to fight on, even after the atomic annihilation of Hiroshima and Nagasaki. One of the final battles of the war was a frantic spat in the grounds of Tokyo's Imperial Palace on 14 August that year, as conspirators tried to seize the recording of the surrender message read by the Shōwa Emperor himself that would be broadcast to the nation the following day. Two men were killed, and a third committed suicide, although it is unclear whether he did so because of the surrender or the failure of the coup attempt. The ringleaders fled on motorcycles, throwing explanatory leaflets through the streets, and then killed themselves.

The Emperor's 'Jewel Voice Broadcast' was baffling to many, and was delivered in clipped, archaic Japanese riddled with poetic circumlocutions. The war situation, the Emperor suggested, 'has progressed not necessarily to Japan's advantage' and it was time for him to do what was right to preserve peace. After his message finished, someone else had to come on air and explain what he had meant. He had pointedly called out the 'new and most cruel bomb' used by the Allies in Hiroshima and Nagasaki, while neglecting to mention Japan's own atomic weapons programme, underway at Tokyo University since 1941.

In the wake of Japan's surrender – signed on the deck of the USS Missouri in Tokyo Bay, beneath the Stars and Stripes that had once flown on Commodore Perry's flagship – Tokyo entered one of the strangest periods of its history. It was no longer the Emperor's city, but the headquarters of the US Occupation of Japan, characterised for much of its seven years by the figure of General Douglas MacArthur. For many residents, of course, simple subsistence was the first priority, although the Occupation era attempted to impose many cultural transformations intended to eradicate 'militarism' from the national consciousness: rewriting the Japanese constitution, decimating the ranks of the imperial family, forcing the Emperor to renounce his godhood, and imposing a series of foreign cultural norms – kissing in films, votes for women and even Disney films. Walt Disney himself sent a young deer to Ueno Zoo in 1951 as a publicity stunt to promote *Bambi*.

Appeasing the Nation

The dealers of the Akihabara arcades flourished as spivs and black marketeers, somehow always able to find some lard fallen from the back of a freight truck, or some mushrooms sourced from a secret mountain cache. American food aid arrived by the shipload, although there was a catch: the Japanese were ultimately expected to reimburse their new rulers for this 'charity', even though a cynic might observe that it amounted to offloading tonnes of surplus American grain on the local market. The Japanese were not all that sure what to do with wheat, and chafed at advertisements that exhorted them to bake bread and biscuits. A more acceptable local alternative came when entrepreneurial hawkers turned the wheat into noodles, boiled in a broth with a variety of odds and ends. None of these ingredients were particularly new – 'Chinese' soup noodles had been sold in Japan for decades – but these post-war ramen, often sold on the streets by returnees from Japan's former possessions in China, soon became a regular sight. A scrap of black-market meat or fat and a scattering of whatever vegetables were to hand, in a piping hot soup, became the default lunch of Japan's working man (see Eating and Drinking).

As food shortages eased, Akihabara adopted a sideline in modern goods. What better place, after all, with the freight trains coming through, to sell electric fans, ice-boxes and (by the late 1950s) transistor radio parts? Just as in its vegetable days, Akihabara became notorious for its fierce competition, as neighbouring dealers fought to undercut each other, sometimes by selling goods that had been obtained through underhand means.

The Occupation era imposed a censorship policy almost as harsh as that of the militarist regime it had supplanted. It launched a ruthless war against references to Japan's past, particularly the samurai elite that it accused of luring the people of Japan into the 'dark valley' of militarism. That was all very well, but the samurai had dominated Japan for a thousand years; Japan's cultural make-up – its artefacts, its historical personages, even its fashions – had been fundamentally steered by the wants and wishes of the military men who had run the nation since the Middle Ages.

Some elements of Japanese culture were only preserved through careful management of expectations and loopholes. Kabuki theatre, which once featured an entire subgenre of modern-dress potboiler plays, improvised overnight and ripped from the newspaper headlines of the day, suddenly concentrated only on the classical repertoire. Martial arts, formerly integrated heavily into the militarised culture of the Empire, were abruptly reinvented as sports or religions that played down the practicalities of knowing how to punch people. The samurai and their modern military successors had dominated Japanese culture for so long that it sometimes seemed impossible to extricate them from it. In a bold move in 1948, an antiquarian society mounted an exhibition of Japanese swords, pleading with visitors to appreciate them not as weapons, but as works of intricate art and exquisite craft. The exhibition was a roaring success, and would eventually grow into the Japanese Sword Museum (see Gazetteer: Sumida).

Temporary housing for the Occupation forces was built near the old imperial army mustering grounds at Harajuku. The district had been flattened and burned to the ground by the wartime air raids, but now flourished as a foreign enclave, known as 'Washington Heights'. Home at that time to hundreds of American army and air force families, Washington Heights no longer exists, but is notable today for its spin-off effect: the hard currency and exotic habits of the American residents fostered a thriving set of businesses nearby that catered to foreign tastes. The trade went both ways, with short-lived but lucrative enterprises springing up to flog tacky souvenirs to the invaders. A more enduring impact was created by the junk shops that harvested the leavings of military families being sent home, creating a market of second-hand records, colourful cast-off clothes and cafés serving foreign foods. Long after the American servicemen had left, Harajuku would remain a touchstone for bricolage and fast fashion.

The samurai past returned to bite the Americans in other ways. In 1945, Occupation forces decided to build a motor pool area near the Imperial Palace. They had plenty of land to choose from, since the firebombings had flattened almost all of the area. They decided to create their jeep- and truck-marshalling zone in Ōtemachi, and sent in a bulldozer crew to sweep out the junk and push aside an earth mound that was in their way. The bulldozer struck the plinth of a stone stele and overturned, killing the driver. A local civil leader rushed over to Occupation headquarters to explain the sensitive nature of Masakado's resting place, which caused the supposedly no-nonsense Americans to backtrack on their plans and instead restore the site to its pre-war glory.

6

The Japanese Miracle: 1952–1989

TO FIND THE MUSEUM, you have to go to the Sompo Insurance Building, which soars above bustling Shinjuku station. Take the elevator to the 42nd floor, where you can view a gallery of some 200 works by the painter Tōgō Seiji (1897–1978), if you can tear yourself away from the vistas of the city outside the windows to look at them. Honoured by the cultural institutions of both Japan and France, where he had studied as a young man and dabbled in Futurism, Tōgō is presumably a draw for a certain faction of Japanese art lovers, although he is unlikely to be the reason that most people visit the museum bearing his name. There are temporary exhibitions that also bring in new visitors – guest collections from Parisian colleagues, or other works by Japanese Modernists. But ask any of the visitors who mill around the collection, and they will tell you they are really there for a trio of European paintings that have pride of place: Paul Gauguin's *Lane at Alchamps, Arles*, depicting a country road near Arles; Paul Cézanne's still life *Apples and Napkin*; and the one that everyone remembers, Vincent van Gogh's metre-high *Vase with Fifteen Sunflowers*.

Van Gogh actually painted a dozen pictures of sunflowers. This particular one features 15 in a vase, and dates from his Arles period, shortly after he had encountered Japanese prints in the midst of the flowering of Parisian *Japonisme*. Its acquisition by a Tokyo corporation was a watershed moment in cultural history, marking the Japanese as the new trendsetters in the art world. For the Tokyo audience, it also had the additional cachet of a wrong righted, since an earlier *Sunflowers* painting by Van Gogh had been destroyed during the bombing of Yokohama in 1945.

Yasuda Fire and Marine Insurance had been double-dipping its investments since 1976, ever since its owners realised that valuable antiques were both useful ways of insulating savings against inflation and also assets in their own right that the public could be charged an admission fee to see. Gotō Yasuo, the company head, was sitting pretty with all the publicity of his purchase, garnering immense marketing capital back in Japan, when he announced that the picture would form part of his company's centenary celebrations – it ended up as his corporate logo. Although the sale of the *Sunflowers* picture was regarded worldwide as a sign of vainglorious excess, the money that the Yasuda corporation sunk into it remained ironically ironclad during the recession that followed. Companies that had invested in overblown Tokyo real estate found their book value plummeting as land prices collapsed. But the value of this rare painting by a world-famous artist continued to rise. Yasuda Fire and Marine was eventually folded into the parcel of companies that makes up today's Sompo conglomerate, but if the corporation's executives ever wanted to liquidate their canvas assets, I dare say that they could find a suitably wealthy buyer in China or Russia who would be prepared to make it worth their while.

The Olympic Dream

It was a long road from the Occupation, which ended in 1952, to the Tokyo Olympics of 1964, with the foreign presence still palpable. The Korean War, the Cold War and the Vietnam War would keep American military bases in Japan, but would also involve the Japanese indirectly in the support industries that made jeeps, trucks and parachutes. These would have unexpected spin-off effects, not only revitalising Japanese industry, but also leading to unusual attempts to repurpose the surplus. The weirdest of these has to be pachinko, the automated urban Japanese pinball phenomenon that created a use for all the ball bearings left over after the Korean War.

The singer Akatsuki Teruko summed up the era with her 1951 song *Tokyo Shoeshine Boy*, an upbeat ditty with a downtrodden message about a Japan that was still in thrall to American dominance. The titular shoeshine boy is getting on with his work, doing his earnest best to make every scrap of leather sparkle, while musing:

> That lady that I like
> Hasn't turned up yet today
> But perhaps she'll come back
> Even if it's rainy or windy.

The girl in question appears to have business elsewhere, as a later verse reveals:

> That lady in red shoes
> Is she back walking around Ginza today
> With gifts of chocolate
> Chewing gum and Coca Cola?

With its recognisable foreign words and its frisky rhythm, *Tokyo Shoeshine Boy* was a hit in the dance halls

– but it is also a flatly hopeless elegy, loaded with subtle clues, starting with the slang term for a Ginza promenade, *Gin-bura*. As the novelist Tanizaki Junichirō once archly observed, only a country hick would use such a phrase. That poor migrant labourer has nothing to offer her – he literally couldn't even shine her red shoes with his boot-black polish, nor can he pile her with presents like GI-issue chocolate and chewing gum, or take her for an exotic Coke in swanky Ginza. 'I'm sure she'll come back tomorrow,' he says brightly. 'Someday we'll go out dancing together.' It is a triumph of Japanese melancholy, never once letting its enthusiasm slip, even though any listener can plainly see what has happened. The song makes background appearances in two films – listen closely and you'll hear it evoking the pop culture of the Korean War in *M*A*S*H*, and playing incongruously during a terrorist attack in *Akira*.

Television arrived in Japan in 1953. The technology would transform the city's skyline. The original transmitter of NHK, Japan's national public broadcaster, was inadequate to cover the entire Kantō region, and rival firms soon popped up with their own broadcast requirements. In order to avoid peppering the entire city with antennae, a consortium of channels and developers pooled their resources to create one massive broadcasting tower with a footprint that would reach all the way to the mountains. Modelled at least superficially on the Eiffel Tower in Paris, Tokyo Tower was originally intended to be taller than New York's Empire State Building, although resources and requirements eventually dictated a slightly shorter height of 332.9 metres.

Work began on the tower in 1957 – the popular 2005–12 film series *Always: Sunset on Third Street* would later use the sight of the tower under construction as a background evocation of life in the post-Occupation period. Tokyo Tower became a symbol of Japan's reconstruction, rising from the ashes of the war-torn city, asserting Japan's greatness in the post-war world, and doing so by quite literally repurposing the trash of the old world order – a full third of the steel used in its construction came from hundreds of scrapped US tanks from the Korean War. It was completed in 1958, proclaimed as the tallest freestanding tower in the world, at least for a while, and painted in a bold orange-and-white colour scheme for safety purposes.

'The fact that the Tokyo Tower is a cultural landmark building,' writes the journalist and author Patrick Macias, 'speaks volumes about the lack of cultural landmark buildings in Tokyo.' It was always intended to have a dual function as a tourist site, although the prospect of having an observation deck a bit higher than the surrounding buildings would diminish in appeal as the years passed. Today, it seems faintly ludicrous to be excited about the prospect of being a few floors up when you've arrived in Tokyo in a jumbo jet. The Foot Town shopping complex beneath lures visitors to stay longer with restaurants and several museums, but, to be brutally frank, the tower never quite achieved the status abroad that its investors had hoped for. Tourist brochures heralding Japan abroad tended to plump for stereotypical scenes depicting natural beauty or evoking the samurai. If they wanted to go modern, they would go for Mount Fuji, foregrounded by a rushing bullet train. The only place that Tokyo Tower achieved significant recognition was among the legions of movie fans who would see it regularly trashed, bent and stomped on by the likes of Godzilla, Mothra and Mechani-Kong. This is particularly ironic, since at least part of the will to destroy the tower on the part of 1960s film-makers surely stemmed from its role serving the competition, broadcasting the TV programmes that were luring audiences away from cinemas.

Tokyo was transformed once more in the 1960s, by virtue of that periodic agent of demolition and reconstruction, the Olympic Games. Washington Heights, at the time still a barracks and prefab housing estate for American servicemen, was finally requisitioned for state use. The surviving ramshackle slums of Harajuku were at last redeveloped as Olympic sites, and much of what had been Washington Heights was repurposed as housing for athletes.

Several highway renewal schemes were brought forward to coincide with the games, along with two new subway lines and the famous Shinkansen (meaning 'New Trunk Line') railway, which initially ran to Ōsaka, but quickly expanded into a network across the country. It was soon known in English by a far more evocative nickname: the Bullet Train.

Sometimes, the building crews would work through the night, obliging local residents to hang heavy black curtains in their windows and sleep wearing earplugs. The frenzy of rebuilding was less obvious in the Marunouchi district, where the proximity of the Emperor's palace kept the new buildings at a maximum of only eight storeys.

It was this period that saw the construction of the Tokyo Expressway, a road project that led to the infilling and permanent loss of several prominent canals – often the easiest route through built-up areas split between hundreds of smallholders. This is the main reason for the large number of place names in Tokyo that come with *-hashi* or *-bashi* suffixes (Shinbashi, Nanbashi, Konya-bashi and so on) denoting now-demolished bridges over canals that no longer exist.

Tange Kenzō (1913–2005), the architect responsible for many of the large Olympic structures that still endure, had other plans for Tokyo. He had already unveiled a plan to expand the city out to sea, colonising the waters of

Tokyo Bay with a road network and zoning for futuristic homes and industries. The plan seems to have been a mere fancy, but it inspired several fictional incarnations. The artist Ōtomo Katsuhiro, a teenager at the time of the Tokyo Olympics, would eventually replicate elements of Tange's proposal in his design for Neo-Tokyo, the megacity location of his landmark manga *Akira*.

Technology continued to transform the Tokyo landscape, and not always for the better in the eyes of its denizens. Since the advent of the tram, and for decades of train and bus travel, on-board ticketing had been in the hands of young, high-school-educated clippies, often the subject of erotic speculation and unwelcome male attention – uniformed public servants, tasked with being polite and friendly, even to old perverts. However, the introduction in the 1960s of the 'one-man bus', operated by a driver alone, put paid to these much-adored conductresses of Japanese public transport.

Akihabara, already established as the place to shop for discount electronics, underwent a new and lasting transformation as a Mecca for computer nerds. Locals, visitors from other parts of Japan and soon even tourists began to regard it as 'Electric Town' – the ideal place to pick up the latest camera, games console or computer, not only as finished products, but in unfinished forms as assorted chips, leads and cables. It retained its old souk-like reputation, but swiftly gained a superstructure of bright neon lights (now LEDs) and blaring pop music. By the late 1980s, Akihabara stores offered not only computer games but also the comics, videos and figurines that enjoyed a symbiotic relationship with them. The *Akiba-kei* (Akiba tribe) started to feature in local media stories that contrasted the 'otaku' nerds of this neighbourhood with the more self-consciously trendy *Shibuya-kei* of nearby Shibuya, which fancied itself as a centre for nightlife and music.

The Oil Shocks

The 1964 Olympics were intended (and recognised) as a restoration of Japan's international reputation, welcoming the foreign community to a land that was trying to forget its martial past. Much of the redevelopment was centred on Tokyo, and so the immediate aftermath of the Olympics was a sheepish refocus on the outer suburbs and the rest of Japan, parts of which had been vocally complaining about the expenditure of so much national funding on a purely localised event. Inspired by the Discover America campaign in the United States, Japanese National Railways began a massive media blitz to stimulate domestic tourism. The Olympics had transformed infrastructure; the 1970 Ōsaka Expo had kept the momentum; but now the onus was on local prefectures to really push Japanese citizens out and about. The aim, of course, was to encourage long train journeys out of Tokyo, but local railways fought back with their own campaigns to create must-see destinations. If there wasn't a suitably historic temple or relaxing spa at the far terminus of a particular line, you could be sure that the railway companies would *make* one.

Some Tokyo areas continued to change after the Olympics. The old Washington Heights barracks area in Harajuku was prettified as Yoyogi Park; a single dwelling from the army days survives in the park grounds, where it has since played witness to many weekend gatherings of trendy young folk from the nearby shopping areas, preening in public and displaying their fashion choices, often in coordinated dance-offs.

Frank Lloyd Wright's three-story Imperial Hotel, once considered an imposing structure, began to seem somewhat dwarfed by the skyscrapers springing up around it. Still suffering the long-term scars of wartime bombing, and subsiding dangerously in some places because of its foundations 'floating' on soft clay, the building was finally demolished in 1967. Its striking entranceway and lobby, however, were carted off to the open-air architectural museum Meiji-Mura, near Nagoya, where they were finally reconstructed in 1985. You can still see them there today.

Belt tightening characterised the 1970s, as all of Japan reeled from the increased price of oil resulting from the global energy crisis. Lacking much in the way of natural resources, Japan was ill prepared for a sudden hike in fuel prices. But ventures continued to improve and augment the city of Tokyo – not always with unmitigated success. As Haneda Airport, built in 1931, was hemmed in by buildings and the shoreline and already unable to expand, the decision was taken to build a bigger airport further out. Narita Airport, in the next-door prefecture of Chiba, was announced in 1966 and was supposed to be finished by 1971. Local farmers had other ideas, protesting about the compulsory purchase of their land, and soon attracted a cloud of radicals, revolutionaries and communists determined to ruin the plans. Some of these new arrivals subscribed to the conspiracy theory that Narita was actually a stealth US airbase, being readied for a war with the Soviet Union. However, after many years of protests, sit-ins and monkey-wrenching, the construction was completed under heavily armed guard, and the airport was opened seven years late. The inaugural ceremony was delayed for a further two months after protestors broke in with a burning car and threw petrol bombs at the control tower.

This has all contributed to a general lack of love felt for Narita Airport, which even today retains over-the-top security measures and heavy fortifications (noticeable in the timorous twenty-first century not for their presence, but for their age) and incurs high landing fees, in part to pay for all this. At 66 kilometres from the centre of Tokyo, it is substantially further out than many other capital-city airports.

The relics of the war came back to haunt Japan, nowhere more noticeably than at the Yasukuni Shrine (see Gazetteer: Chiyoda), founded in 1869 by the Meiji Emperor to heal internal wounds. The shrine's original conciliatory purpose had transformed throughout the late nineteenth and early twentieth centuries, as its Book of Souls turned into an ongoing and ever-growing memorial listing the names of the fallen in Japan's overseas wars of conquest. By the 1940s, the Yasukuni Shrine was, at least on paper, playing host to the spirits of more than two million soldiers. Baulking at the military tone of its relics, and keen to find a patch of ground to erect a dog-racing track, the US Occupation force had considered razing the whole thing to the ground, only to be dissuaded by two Catholic priests, Bruno Bitter and Patrick Byrne, who argued that every nation should be allowed to mourn its war dead. Yasukuni was allowed to survive and was granted protection as a 'religious' building in 1946. Notably, its grounds include sub-shrines to not only Japan's fallen, but also loyal soldiers from Japan's colonies, as well as an all-encompassing memorial to anyone who dies as a result of conflict. You might think that this would all sound completely innocent, but it has become something of a cause célèbre.

Much as Winston Churchill has a memorial in Westminster Abbey, the Yasukuni Shrine acknowledges Japan's wartime prime minister, Tōjō Hideki. Tōjō was executed as a class-A war criminal, and yet the phrasing of Shintō rituals, particularly in translation, implies that anyone venerated at Yasukuni has been turned into a 'god' – including a dozen of Tōjō's class-A colleagues, and a thousand other figures who were indicted as war criminals in the post-war purges. This is very much a sub-version of the shrine's original intent, and has turned it into a political hot potato for both the left and right in the post-war period. Anti-war activists regard Yasukuni as a venue that glorifies Japan's imperialist expansion; the far right see it as a temple to noble soldiery, and it is this latter faction that seems to have won the battle over how the shrine presents itself.

Yasukuni is a thorny ideological problem, and one's reaction to it very much depends on where one comes down on war in general. It has hence become a touchstone of Japanese pride and revisionist fervour. Almost every Japanese prime minister since 1945 has made a point of visiting it as a means of currying favour with the right and standing up to foreign powers. In 1980, Pope John Paul II tried to defuse its status (or possibly stoke its controversies) by pointedly saying a Mass on behalf of all its souls. Both Yasukuni and its nearby museum, the Yūshūkan, predictably avoid a lot of the discussions of blame and guilt one might expect to find in, say, a museum about the Holocaust. Instead, they all too readily present Japan and the Japanese as unwitting victims in an imperialist setup, lured into war by conniving foreigners and made to suffer a bitter brand of victor's justice.

In some cases, such commentary can be fascinating – it is through Yasukuni, for example, that many tourists first become acquainted with the Indian judge Radhabinod Pal (1886–1967), the lone dissenting voice at the post-war trials. He opposed the very notion of class-A criminality, raised the issue of 'victor's justice' and protested that many Japanese were being held to account for newly invented crimes that were alien to them. But even Pal's incendiary comments, which ran to a legal argument of over a thousand pages, have been simplified and twisted by Yasukuni signage to say things that he did not really mean. Wherever one stands on Japan's wartime record – the abuses of prisoners of war, the rationale for Hiroshima, false surrenders and suicide attacks – you can be sure that the Yasukuni Shrine exhibits will take things too far for comfort. Most notoriously, the museum goes out of its way to insist that the Rape of Nanjing – in which Japanese soldiers massacred tens of thousands of Chinese men, women and children – never happened.

The Bubble Era

Strictly speaking, the term 'Bubble era' refers to the rapid expansion of the Japanese economy between 1986 and 1989, when the yen could seemingly do no wrong, and Japanese purchasing power abroad reached the insane levels required to buy Van Gogh paintings as investments. But popular usage often winds it all the way back to the late 1970s, as Japan pulled itself out of the oil shocks and began to enjoy meteoric economic success in consumer electronics. Japan came to reap the benefits of its workers' long struggle through difficult conditions and uncivil working hours to create a booming economy, and the long-standing effects of industrial schemes to make not only hardware, but also the software that played on it – the first rumblings of 'Cool Japan'. This has become increasingly important for tourists in Tokyo, as the city ceases to be a place where history happened to other people, and becomes more like the setting where so many beloved movies, stories or computer games unfolded for the generation raised on Sony, Nintendo and Sega.

Hirohito, the Shōwa Emperor, died in January 1989, shortly before the economic slump that would put a punctuation mark at the end of his era. The Japanese had mixed feelings about the departure of the man who had been the imperial figurehead since becoming his ailing father's regent in 1921. Even as mourning crowds lined the roads to watch his cortège pass by, and the media piously marked the occasion with solemn music, 100,000 people gathered at protest rallies across the city to denounce him as a war criminal. Rarely mentioned today in jumpy anti-terror times is the fact that several explosive devices went off around the city, including at the Tōgō Shrine in Shibuya.

Fittingly, perhaps, for an era that derives its name from an effervescent sphere comprising nothing but air, the Bubble era is hard to see directly in contemporary Tokyo. It remains, however, a vital contributor to the modern visitor's experience of the city, in part for the huge amount of wealth that was briefly squirrelled away in antiquities and assets. The fact that Tokyo today boasts over 160 museums is itself partly a legacy of the Bubble era, when many corporations saw fit to write off profits in charitable ventures, or to create sites of cultural interest in a scramble to put their shopping malls ahead of their competitors' in the struggle to attract customers. True enough, many innovations were matters of miniaturisation like the Walkman, turning the experience of the city dweller in on itself, transforming the architecture of public spaces, such as restaurants, away from tables facing a table full of fellow human beings towards stools facing a window on the world outside. Its most enduring image can still be seen today, although it is not strictly speaking *of* the Bubble era alone: the Shibuya 'pedestrian scramble', the busiest road crossing in the world, dominated by massive TV screens, where a bustle of commuters charge in multiple directions across a major intersection. The sight is weirdly compelling, and has become evocative for many visitors of the Tokyo experience: hordes of people on their way to somewhere else, obligingly obeying the signs until the lights change, unheeding of where they are, focused on some other goal, and yet unwittingly forming an unforgettable part of the landscape. Unlike many other Tokyo sights, witnessing this teeming mass on the move is also free of charge.

Such simple pleasures became sought after by increasing numbers of Tokyo residents as the Bubble era popped and Japan was plunged into two decades of austerity. The most recent developments in the city have reflected this fact – that much of what makes Tokyo appeal to visitors has been unexpected, and something of a subversion of what its town planners were expecting. But Tokyo continues to pivot with the times, and offers new experiences for a new century.

7

Austerity Tokyo: 1989–2019

H ER NAME IS LUM and she is out of this world. The
statue is sitting daintily on a bench, her right hand
pointing nowhere in some kind of sci-fi gang sign, her
booted legs kicking up in the air as if she were weight-
less. Her features – huge eyes and a tiny button nose, her
mouth little more than a blank 'O' in her face – would be
distractingly alien to people of any earlier age. And she
appears to be wearing a tiger-striped bikini.

The alien Lum first appeared in Takahashi Rumiko's
1978 manga *Urusei Yatsura*, in which, owing to a series
of misunderstandings, she ended up sort-of engaged to
Ataru, a lecherous loser from Nerima who is obliged
to literally keep her in his closet while the problem is
untangled. With brash, liberal cluelessness, Lum parades
around in a skimpy tiger-skin bikini, electrocutes anyone
who gets too close to her and grows horns and fangs of
jealousy if any woman gets too close to her witless man.

Lum got her name from the real-world model Agnes
Lum (b.1956), a busty Chinese-Hawaiian girl who shot
to fame at a critical meeting of technologies – quality
photography, full-colour printing and cheaper air travel.
She became one of the stars of Japan's *gravure* photography culture – or, as a cynic might rephrase it, the perfect
excuse for ageing photographers to claim on expenses for

a trip to a beach resort with a hot girl in a bikini. One can sense, in Takahashi's depiction of her, a little bit of eye-rolling exasperation with the easily pleased male gaze, and frustration with women only ever being rated on their appearance. Like the real Lum, the cartoon Lum is an alien figure, a bit of eye candy for the Japanese male to lust over before he sees sense and marries the Japanese 'girl next door'.

The cartoon Lum's existence as a statue, however, post-dates the comic and cartoon series that made her famous. She's just one of many characters celebrated in the pedestrian thoroughfare known as the Ōizumi Anime Gate. Back in the 1980s, city planners scoffed at the very idea of such a commemoration. 'At the time, no local community was serious about constructing a prominent statue of a cartoon character,' a staffer from another anime studio confessed to the *Asahi Shimbun* newspaper. 'There was opposition to the plan, saying it would make the city a laughing stock.'

How times change. Tokyo in the twenty-first century is often a monument to its own mythologies, a constant carnival of photo opportunities. This in turn reflects the gradual realisation, enshrined in government policy around 2005, that even as Japan's heavy industries were taking a nosedive in the face of foreign competition, losing their edge as they became multinational corporations that no longer offered employment to Japanese workers, Japan's *soft* power was a global phenomenon. The hardware might now be made in Malaysia or Thailand, but the software was still indelibly Japanese. Japanese movies were escaping from the bargain bins; Japanese comics and cartoons were consumed around the world; an entire generation of children around the world had been reared in front of PlayStations, Sega consoles and Nintendo Game Boys.

Where pilgrims once stamped their notebooks with proofs of having visited all the temples in a particular series of excursions, modern-day travellers visit film locations where their movie icon lovers first kissed or caught a bad guy. They take selfies running in mock terror from a Godzilla statue, or pose boldly in front of a life-sized giant robot. Such transformations in the city's fortune are, it has to be said, liable to be short-term fads. In many cases, they are already a form of legacy management, trying to wring the last in recognition and consumption from franchises that are already ageing and, in the case of many of the Nerima statues, already forgotten by the young.

In part due to the well-intentioned chauvinism of Confucianism – which advocates keeping women out of sight, and not speaking the name of a lady in public – very few of the public monuments to important historical figures are sculptures of real women. Most of the statues in Tokyo depict men – warriors, statesmen and politicians of the samurai era, selected by well-meaning and man-heavy committees. There are millions of cartoon miniatures of women in kit and resin form, of course, scattered throughout the shops of Akihabara and the bedrooms of the suburbs, but remarkably few women are afforded the chance to claim a public space as their own, to stare across the waters of a fountain at office workers eating their packed lunches, and dare them to wonder why they are there. Even Kannon, the Goddess of Mercy, originated in India as a man and somehow changed sex on the journey. Even Hachikō the dog was male.

The Japanese print world, on the other hand, is brimming with women, mainly idealised and sexually available beauties, scary psychopaths, repressed housewives and the ever-present schoolgirls. Since the Bubble era, women have also been the implied targets of much Japanese domestic tourist literature. The archetype of a 'parasite single' (their term, not mine!), a low-level office lady sponging off her parents while waiting for Mr Right, has become the focus of much of the marketing of branded goods, perfumes and indeed travel. The expectations of tourist authorities' functions are changing, so that they need to serve shoppers above all else. This has created something of a split between assumptions about foreign and domestic tourists in Japan. You, dear reader, might be coming to see the history of Tokyo, but many Japanese travellers are seemingly expected to travel to experience the immediate moment, spending their money not on cultural pursuits but on consumption. That, at least, is the impression I get from many of the Japanese-language books I have read about Tokyo. There are, of course, some that continue to hunt down temples and old-city walks, but the most common images are of shopping arcades and the SkyTree.

Skyscrapers and the SkyTree

The Bank of Japan intervened in the Bubble on 31 December 1989, belatedly raising interest rates and bringing the artificially inflated land prices tumbling down. The Bubble burst, leading to chain reactions as entire conglomerates discovered that their multi-million-yen loans to each other trailed back to parcels of land that could not possibly be sold off to clear the debts. Banks failed; factories closed. Japan's 'just-in-time' system, outsourcing many elements of industry to smaller companies and suppliers, was suddenly lacking crucial links in the manufacturing process. Many familiar brands survived by pivoting offshore, relocating to elsewhere in East Asia, and even setting up car plants in America and electronics assembly lines in Europe – but that was no good to the

Tokyo labourer. Workers who had believed their jobs were guaranteed for life were suddenly edged into constructive dismissal. Ageing executives were reassigned to work as human traffic cones, or given impossibly Herculean tasks designed to force their resignation. The effect was most powerful on the young, who had been struggling through the strict education system, only to discover a constricted job market on graduation. Movies and novels about the 1980s depict the era as a gilded dream-time of beautiful people and infinite resources, as viewed from a dingy, cramped bedsit before an alarm wakes the occupant up for the long commute to a McJob.

In the meantime, Japan's corporations came up with moneymaking schemes. Nothing, it seems, was safe. The Mitsui Finance Corporation even embarked on a controversial effort to sell mineral mining rights to a parcel of land in Ōtemachi in central Tokyo, even though the land in question included the grave mound and shrine of a familiar famous figure from Tokyo's past: Masakado. In 2002, the corporation suddenly and surprisingly filed for bankruptcy. Possibly this was a logical outcome of the straitened financial circumstances that had led its accountants to try to sell the mining rights, but the population of Tokyo saw it differently. Urban myth soon attributed the company's misfortune to yet another iteration of the curse of Masakado, fiercely defending his last resting place in the middle of Tokyo.

It was not lost on some of Japan's policymakers that cultural exports were a valuable form of capital. Intellectual property could be sold and sold again. Films and TV shows made in Japan could function as advertisements for the places they depicted, fostering a new facet of the tourist industry. Instead of favouring Mount Fuji, or the temples of Kyōto, perhaps a new class of hipster tourist could be encouraged to visit the station exit where the two star-crossed lovers in a certain movie said their good-byes, or the road crossing where Godzilla once stamped on a tank.

This market sector was openly identified in 2005, when the Nomura Research Institute published *Otaku Marketing*, a prophetic outline of the kind of media we take for granted today, with an emphasis on 'collection, creativity and community'. In the future year of 2020, its authors imagined, a lucrative growth area in tourism and merchandise would favour the customisable, narrowcast experience of a certain kind of fan, seeking out unique experiences that mirrored their media-watching habits. In particular, the anime and manga worlds came to develop a subgenre of *nichijō* (everyday) storylines, designed to reflect slices of real life in Japan. Abroad, however, the differences between 'everyday' in Tokyo and everywhere else would make trips to Japan seem like a science-fictional experience for many a media fan. 'Come to Tokyo,' they might say. 'They've got coffee in cans and capsule hotels, cat cafés and bowing robots.'

Flushed with enthusiasm after Expo '85 in Tsukuba across the bay, the Tokyo government had poured money into its harbour district, announcing a huge docklands renewal initiative in which a graceful bridge would connect the city proper to the low-lying plots of reclaimed land at the bayside. The portside development of the artificial island Odaiba was expected to be a fantastic opportunity for business real estate, and hence became one of the most infamous white elephants of the collapse of the Bubble economy, resulting by the mid-1990s in a windswept wasteland. Canny officials rezoned it for commerce and entertainment in 1996, and Odaiba swiftly mushroomed into a high-tech playground, helped greatly by the inauguration that year of Tokyo Big Sight, the country's largest exhibition and conference centre.

Fuji TV, which opened its quirky new headquarters nearby in 1997, wasted no time in making the area the location for *Bayside Shakedown*, its big cop-show hit of the decade. Considering that Odaiba was nothing but 'for sale' signs and billboards barely a generation ago, the area has become over-represented in Japanese media ever since, both as a location for TV shoots (especially for Fuji) and as a magnet for conference-goers and the attendant press coverage that their events draw in. Statistically, it plays host to one of the largest throughputs of Tokyo visitors, although the Tokyo those visitors see is relentlessly, unapologetically modern.

Ever since the post-war reconstruction era, such megaprojects have been the engine that drives the Tokyo economy. Coalitions of the construction, rail and property industries create their own mini towns, crossing their fingers that something about their venture will lure customers away from rivals. But such decade-long ventures also bring an orbiting cloud of smaller-time speculators, hoping to capitalise on the larger customer traffic coming to see the main attraction. Blueprints are closely guarded, and the precise locations of the station exits often kept secret, in order to prevent wily would-be barkeepers and shopkeepers snapping up cheap land that will soon rise in value if it turns out to be close to a hole in the ground that vomits thousands of customers every day.

Modern Tokyo speculators obsess over such portents like Londoners discussing their mortgages. Murakami Haruki, who had a jazz bar in Tokyo before he found fame as a novelist, once even posed as a student of railway history in an attempt to befriend the planner who knew where the exits would be placed on a new station. Some people, however, have made their own luck, even in the recession. The business tycoon Mori Minoru had been buying plots of land in Roppongi since 1989, swooping in to snatch them as the prices continued to fall. He spent 14 years amassing his patch of the city, before he was able to conflate 400 separate locations into a single massive building site. Not every resident was willing to vacate their property, but Mori's corporation was granted the power of eminent domain, effectively enabling it to force the last stragglers off the land – although Mori had to buy them off with the promise of apartments when his project was finished. The result, opening in 2003, was the Roppongi Hills development, topped by the soaring Mori Tower. Mori's argument, common to many an urban developer, was that it was futile to commute for an hour into town, when you could live *above* it and commute down in just minutes.

Behind the scenes, another invisible technological transformation would spell disaster for a Tokyo landmark. With tourist attendance already dropping, Tokyo Tower was found to be no longer fit for its main purpose as a TV broadcast antenna. The new requirements of all-digital broadcasting, and the obstructions caused by multiple skyscrapers all over the city, now demanded an even larger broadcast tower.

The Tobu Railway company jumped at the chance to meet that need. Its managers had found themselves lumbered with a tempting piece of real estate – a derelict cargo yard, left over from the pre-highway days when Tokyo's construction boom required the movement of building materials by rail. Now, with lorries fulfilling such functions, and passenger traffic lured away by more convenient stations nearby, Tobu needed something to fill the 60,000-square-metre space. A combined subway station, shopping mall and landmark TV tower would do the trick, with the project getting underway in 2005.

In Japan's stagnating economy, there were few excuses for such boondoggles – but the new digital broadcast tower would prove to be an exception. Opened to the public in 2012, the new 634-metre building was named by a public vote. Rejected names included the Edo Tower, evocative of the samurai past, and the Rising East Tower, alluding to the 'Pacific Century' – a term denoting the idea that the twenty-first century will be economically dominated by states of the Asia-Pacific region. One suspects that the architect was rather hoping for the chosen name to be Musashi, which is simultaneously an old word for the Tokyo area, the name of a famous samurai and a punning pronunciation based on the tower's height: 634 metres = *mu-sa-shi*. Inexplicably, the winning name was the meaningless Tokyo SkyTree; we should count ourselves lucky that nobody suggested Buildy McBuilding. As with Tokyo Tower in earlier generations, the structure itself was merely a beacon on top of a more traditional property, in this case the Solamachi ('Sky Town') shopping centre, which also hosts the Sumida Aquarium, a planetarium and the Postal Museum, along with offices and restaurants. In the usual shuffling of place names and associations associated with Tokyo, the nearby Narihira-bashi metro station was renamed Tokyo SkyTree – its fourth name in only a century of operation.

Holy Lands

Japan in 2011 was barely limping out of two lost decades of, if not true recession, then certainly 'stagflation', when the country was hit by a triple whammy: the Tōhoku Earthquake; its subsequent tsunami that wrought such damage to the north of the country; and the attendant disaster at the damaged Fukushima nuclear power plant. The government answered in the only way it really could, by upping already heavy value-added-tax burdens. While the Japanese had been exhorted since 2001 to spend their pocket money at home, the government continued to push initiatives to encourage foreign visitors, since the tax collected from them would not deduct from the spending power of Japanese citizens.

The international community threw Japan a lifeline in the form of the 2020 Olympic Games, which were sure to justify a series of infrastructure schemes that would create jobs in Japan's construction sector. The rather optimistic marketing for the 2020 games promises robot tour guides, real-time translation software for 27 languages, driverless taxis, hydrogen-fuelled energy plants and a maglev train to Nagoya, presumably for people who want to escape. However, the most conspicuous architectural project arising before the Olympics was a matter not of construction but of deconstruction, when the Sony Corporation announced it would demolish its flagship Ginza headquarters. Although a replacement building is scheduled to open in the same location in 2022, the corporation sought to make some marketing capital out of it by turning the site into a park until after the Olympics. What could possibly be a more flashy use of the brand's capital than building an empty public space, albeit a temporary one, right in the middle of the most expensive street in Tokyo?

Part of the city's bid to host the games was a major element of Tokyo that is difficult to see in photographs – a kindness towards visitors that the tourist board hoped to foster in all residents. In her pitch to International Olympic Committee voters in 2013, the French-Japanese TV personality Christel Takigawa introduced the world to the concept of *omotenashi* – kindness for the sake of kindness. Her argument was that visitors to the Tokyo Olympics would be enveloped in a warm embrace of unsolicited aid – lost properties returned, and visitors carefully directed to their destinations. Everybody has a story about the little Japanese old lady who went out of her way to show a baffled gaijin the correct station exit, and Takigawa explained that this was actually a cultural thing. Five years later, an article in *Nikkei Business* called it a lie – a made-up concept that relegated foreign visitors to clueless children who needed to be babied and cosseted around the inscrutable Japanese city, lest they go off like bombs of ignorant frustration. *The Japan Times* summarised the controversy:

> While nearly half – 48.7 percent – of the 1,036 non-Japanese surveyed by *Nikkei Business* stated the level of service in Japan was superior to other countries, and another 35.3 percent agreed it was 'probably better,' large percentages of customers were nevertheless not impressed, and sometimes irritated, by various aspects of service.... Foreign nationals especially disliked being asked personal questions, such as where they came from, while they were in the process of shopping, since such questions were seen as 'irrelevant'.

Tokyo residents, it seems, can't win. They leave foreigners to it, and they are accused of inhabiting a closed, unfathomable society. They try to be nice and they are accused of micro-aggression and insincerity. I've certainly had my fair share of this. I was refused service at the Shinkansen ticket window and directed to the English-speaking office, because foreigners cannot possibly be expected to buy a one-way ticket to Nagoya, even though I have been speaking Japanese since before the ticket seller was even born. Try to remember that, as in many other parts of the Far East, your interactions with locals are part of a complex social contract – the girl at the English window will lose face if her services are not required on the one day a week that a foreigner breezes in. If people are reluctant to talk to you, it is because they are afraid *they* will lose face if they are unable to help. If they seem overly keen to get you to your destination, it is because by even starting to help you, they have obliged themselves to complete the task.

For the historian, such faff is a living relic of the samurai era, when the Japanese were forced to live in close quarters with people who held the power of life and death; contracts were often unwritten; and debts were repaid at long intervals. It made sense then that all interactions should end in harmony and happiness – look, everybody is smiling, let's solve the problem together. I often find that Japanese interactions make a lot more sense if you just pretend that everybody is armed and you just want to get out alive.

The Nomura Research Institute's *Otaku Marketing* outlined transformations in the expectations of consumers and visitors, suggesting that modern culture needed to hatch new experiences: 'events', which created target destinations for fans of a particular hobby, be it photography or car racing or travel itself; 'legends', which promised physical interactions and photo ops with recognisable figures; and 'holy lands' (*seichi*), which turned real-world locations into tourist destinations, often because of their fictional associations. This might seem like common sense today – and, indeed, the Nomura Research Institute was reacting to a trend that was already underway. But the report became a playbook for everybody else, seized with enthusiasm and precision, in complete contrast to attitudes a generation earlier. Where stuffy local officials once scoffed at the idea of a Gundam statue or a Godzilla head peeking from the top of a building, tourist offices have now become intimately entwined with entertainment, as they struggle to encourage film-makers to site their climactic scenes on the observation deck of the Tokyo Tower, or near the statue of Hachikō, or in the foyer of a particular hotel.

For the fan of Japanese culture, this can result in the most bespoke of Tokyo experiences. Your trip to Japan's capital can transform into a tour of all the locations featured in *Tokyo Love Story* or *Your Name*. You can hunt Pokémon in the streets of Shinjuku. Your phone can be pre-loaded with an audio tour that springs into life when shown unobtrusive QR codes stuck to statues and bridges. For the more casual tourist attempting to wander off the beaten track, it can feel like being invited to a party that requires homework. *Why* are there statues of cartoon characters like Lum in Nerima (see Gazetteer: Northern Suburbs)? For an extra level of alienation and bafflement, try wandering a holy land that means nothing to you, like the Shibamata tourist trail that expects visitors to have seen all 48 of the *Otoko ga Tsurai yo* (*It's Tough to be a Man*) 'Tora-san' movies (see Gazetteer: Eastern Suburbs).

It remains possible to ignore this overlay of virtual realities and artificial experiences, and to go in search of shadows of Tokyo's actual history. You can still find its shrines wedged in between car parks, or under staircases that lead to burger bars. You can still duck out of a garish, hyper-enthusiastic product launch and walk a quiet street, past impeccable topiary and trees that are plainly loved, and catch a moment of Tokyo life not all that different from those once reported by Isabel Anderson over a century ago.

I take the Tokyo subway to Ōtemachi station and head out of exit C4, signposted as the way to the Imperial Palace. The area is full of construction hoardings, as an entire city block of skyscrapers is underway. White boards hide every patch of land, except one: a little garden with a couple of trees, one last patch of green in the business district. It is a small square, set behind low walls topped with sculpted privet hedges. There, set upon a triple-stepped plinth, a slab of stone carved with ornate cursive Japanese and images of frogs announces the Buddhist name of a departed samurai. This is all that is left of Masakado's resting place, a tiny scrap of the old world, nestled within the cracks of the new.

8

Eating and Drinking

T OKYO IS A FOODIE'S PARADISE, with all the trappings of a metropolitan capital city, and high scores everywhere for fine dining. Japanese-language guides to Tokyo do go on at length about the great Japanese food to be had there, but devote equal time to the many foreign cuisines on offer – for the Japanese tourist, Tokyo is the place to try artisanal hamburgers, French pastries, authentic Indian curry and outrageously sugary desserts. Then again, so is every other big city in Japan. Try to avoid the hotel restaurants – not because they are going to have substandard food, but because the prices will reflect a captive audience of businessmen on expense accounts and wedding parties trying to impress the in-laws. You end up paying through the nose for the chance to imply that you eat like this all the time.

Food

As a Buddhist island nation with very little land suitable for pasture, Japan has long favoured a diet that is relatively low in meat. Although strict Buddhists and many Buddhist priests avoided all meat, throughout Japanese history this prohibition has largely been taken to refer to mammals, and so 'fish' (including whales – it's complicated) were exempt.

Fish is a staple of most meals, and often forms the basis of boiling stock (strict vegetarians should enquire) whereas meat and dairy are relatively recent exotica, barely possible before the opening up of the plains of distant Hokkaidō barely 200 years ago. Before then, meat was usually only eaten for medicinal purposes. 'Traditional' food is hence usually reflective of the samurai-era farm or fishing village, while recent imports can be identified by their foreign names, like *suteeki* (steak), *biifu* (beef), or *katsu* (cutlet). Chicken was frowned upon for a long time, but started cropping up in Japanese cookbooks in the seventeenth century.

Edomae-zushi (morsels from [the bay] before Edo) was the old Tokugawa-era name for the bite-sized snacks that capitalised on the city's proximity to rice farms and fresh fish. Today, as just plain **sushi**, it has become one of Japan's great exports to the world. The best way to try it is at a conveyor-belt sushi bar, or *kaiten*, where language barriers and general confusion evaporate because the food itself drifts past you at regular intervals while you pluck up the courage to try it. *Kaiten* usually charge by the plate – get used to the games the system plays with you, eking out the cheap varieties like the cucumber *kappa-maki* in the hope you will give up waiting and snatch a more expensive sea urchin or abalone. The ginger slices are to cleanse your palette between dishes. The soy sauce and hot wasabi paste are to be used sparingly. The posher the sushi restaurant, the more gauche it will appear if you decide to add seasoning to something that the chef has already carefully prepared. By all means, dip away in a *kaiten*, with the sushi fish-side down if you really must, but if an earnest chef is offering you bespoke handrolls it's best to trust his judgement and avoid meddling. Technically, sushi comes with vinegary rice; **sashimi** is literal raw fish. That boisterous '*irasshaimase*' greeting from the

staff on arrival is a Tokyo thing – although the custom
has spread elsewhere in the Japanese retail sector and all
over the world's sushi bars, it was originally regarded in
south Japan as yet another example of how uncouth the
Shōgun's capital was.

Curry has maritime and summertime associations for
the Japanese. It was copied by the Imperial Japanese Navy
in the 1870s from the British, who served it as a stew on
their ships to hold off beriberi disease – Japan's Maritime Self-Defense Force still has 'Curry Fridays'. Among
the general population, the hot dish is often served in
summer, because it aids perspiration. Two corporations
dominate the sale of curry sauce in Japan: House Foods,
with its Java and Vermont brands, began trading in 1926;
Spice & herB, counterintuitively abbreviated as S&B,
was the first to use the innovative dissolvable block form
in 1956 – the weird S&B contraction dates from 1949,
and was intended to evoke Britain's Crosse & Blackwell
(C&B), known in pre-war Japan for its curry powder.
However, what passes for curry in Japan is far removed
from the Indian original. Rash Behari Bose (1886–1945)
was an Indian revolutionary exile who married a Japanese
baker's daughter and introduced a more authentic curry
to Japan – his 'Chicken Indian Curry' is still served off
the bone at the Nakamuraya Manna restaurant in Shinjuku. For those that insist on curry as a test of endurance,
the CoCo Ichibanya chain offers strengths rated from
one (mild) to ten (you're kidding), and wisely suggests on
its menus that nobody orders the higher numbers until
they have survived a five. It is delicious, but grades eight
to ten seem pointlessly and unpleasantly hot.

An entire subset of Japanese food dates back to the
previous foreign incursion: the **Nanban** ('Southern
Barbarian') cuisine of the south during the brief sixteenth-
century heyday of contacts with foreign missionaries and

traders. **Tenpura** (tempura), widely thought of as quintessentially Japanese, derives its name from the Portuguese for seasoning. Sugar cane was one of the commodities traded in Nagasaki from the South Seas, leading to **konpeito** sugar candies (from the Portuguese *confeito*) and *castella* sponge cake (from *pão de Castela*). Even the word in Japanese for bread, **pan**, derives from Portuguese.

Other foreign foods have had a strong influence on Japan, particularly French bread and German beer. It would be remiss not to observe the influence of the United States, not merely in the relics of the Occupation era, but in the soft power exerted by franchises like McDonald's, Starbucks and KFC. The latter, in particular, has been peculiarly engaging with its Japanese customers, and has somehow persuaded them that a trip to KFC is a mandatory Christmas tradition. Japan has its own fast-food franchises, notably the for-completists-only Mos Burger and the far nicer Yoshinoya *donburi* chain.

Japan has an odd relationship with Chinese food, not least because some of its signature dishes purportedly originate in the Chinatowns of Yokohama and Nagasaki, while the majority of Japanese 'traditional' foods can trace at least part of their origins back to continental contacts since the Tang dynasty. In fact, the story comes much closer to modern times – the first 'Chinese' restaurant in Tokyo did not open until 1883. Chinese food itself was often regarded with disdain before the 1920s, when Japan's colonial acquisitions in China and Korea brought in a new wave of café owners and street vendors pushing authentic mainland cuisine. As so often happens, the colonised became the colonisers, and much of Japanese 'fast food' is a hybrid with distant roots in what was once the Japanese Empire.

Matters were confused in the post-war period, when American food aid arrived in the form of wheat.

Disregarding Occupation exhortations to get into bread or biscuits, the Japanese instead embraced a new form of Chinese noodle with gusto, serving it in an oily broth hot enough to disinfect the grubbiest of bowls and scattered with a tiny handful of contraband vegetables or black-market meat chunks. Since several previous labels were discounted for being either too pro-Chinese or too racist, the name that was eventually settled on was **ramen**, a vague copy of the Chinese *lamian* – 'pulled noodles'. It is a source of constant surprise, to me at least, how large the bowls are. Ramen were intended as hearty fare for labourers, and are still served accordingly. A few Tokyo cafés have begun offering dainty portions *onna datte* (for the ladies), but the average noodle bar prides itself on serving an entire meal in a bowl and has no time for such scrimping. The female market is largely lost to more upscale restaurants, anyway.

Connoisseurs will tell you that there are rules to ramen cookery almost as elaborate as the rules for sushi. Ignore them, as they are liable to be parroting the claims made in Itami Jūzō's satirical 1985 film *Tampopo*, in which a bunch of losers condescendingly explain the secrets of fast food to an earnest noodle seller. It is difficult to get bad ramen in Japan – the broth should always be piping hot; the ingredients always fresh and in proportion. Unlike in China, where the soup is usually left, it is considered perfectly fine for Japanese ramen eaters to drink the broth – mainland visitors since medieval times have scoffed at Japanese 'beggar's manners', not just in terms of draining one's bowl, but in lifting it off the table when eating. Don't be surprised, either, if there is a lot of slurping going on around you – the sucking action helps cools the noodles, and is a sign of appreciation that suggests to all around you that you are so keen to eat the noodles that you can't wait for the broth to cool down.

Many well-known modern noodle brands come from Japan, and hence have often effectively exported a Chinese commodity back to its homeland. Among the major varieties, **somen**, made from wheat, derive their name from the Chinese *su mian* (basic noodles) and have been around for 2,000 years. Noodles made from winter-crop buckwheat flour flourished in the Tokugawa period and are hence a Tokyo 'tradition', even though buckwheat was itself a medieval import. The grain is called *qiaomai* in Chinese, and **soba** is a Japanese mangling of its medieval pronunciation. **Udon** arrived around the same time, deriving its name from the Chinese *mo tun* (bun dumpling), because these thicker succulent noodles evolved from dumpling skins or similar ravioli-like forms. The glutinous, wriggly **shirataki** (white waterfall) noodles appear to be an actual Japanese invention, deriving from the root vegetable konjac, known as white yam or devil's tongue yam. Another common use for dough in street food is **tako-yaki** (literally 'octopus-fried'), which are round balls of dough with a single garnish in their centre – usually a scrap of sausage or the original octopus.

Even simpler, and often more readily available than even noodles, are the various **donburi** meals – sticky rice with a single topping. *Gyūdon* (cow bowl) was the first recognisable iteration, arriving in 1862 when a Nihonbashi food seller started offering a cut-price dish of a few scraps of beef sprinkled on top of a bed of rice. The cheeky bluntness of the name was copied with the faintly creepy *oyakodon* (parent-child bowl), which pairs the rice with chicken and egg. Many other *don* have since arisen, including *butadon* (pig bowl), *unadon* (eel bowl) and *tendon* (a slightly confusing one, but actually simply 'tempura bowl').

A more distinctly Japanese food is **okonomiyaki** (meaning 'grilled how you like it') in which a cabbage-rich pancake, often fried in front of you on the counter, is finished with a local topping. There is fierce in-fighting among foodies about where this dish originated. There is a Hiroshima style, an Ōsaka style, a whole bunch of regional variants, but the Tokyo style is *monjayaki*, an archaic name for the dish implying, to me at least, that Tokyo was the default setting. An Asakusa vendor of *okonomiyaki* is noted in reportage as early as 1937, but these are fighting words to the people of Ōsaka, who say they thought of it, and the people of Hiroshima, who say they perfected it. As with many Tokyo traditions, it is difficult to work out whether a regional style was appropriated and popularised in the capital, or simply arose there.

Hotpot dishes – the savoury **sukiyaki** and the sweeter **shabu-shabu** – stew meat slices and vegetables in a broth. Food historians also argue about the origins of these dishes; some Japanese claim that they are farmhouse traditions, while others date their arrival to late in the Meiji period. I am tempted to point out that the very similar *huoguo* (hotpot) has been common in China since the Middle Ages and that, disregarding nuances in broth and ingredients, the whole setup owes much of its appeal and endurance to the disinfectant qualities of boiling water, and the social capital of huddling around a warm bowl of communal food.

One of the surprising changes in Japanese cuisine in the twenty-first century has been caused by the vast influx of Chinese tourists. Japanese food of Chinese origin is the basis of most 'local' cuisine, but explicitly 'Chinese' food was once downmarket and low in quality. Even ten years ago 'Chinese food' in Japan was a ghastly procession of greasy rubbish, but restaurants that cater to the Chinese themselves, and hence have to pass proper muster, have since improved the quality immensely. You can still get a sense of Japanised Chinese food in any ramen bar, where *cha han* (fried rice) or gyōza (fried dumplings) are sure to be on the menu.

A word to the wise – the most dangerous food in Japan is not, as some believe, the meat of the fugu blow-fish, which carries with it a light sauce of its own poison, sufficient to induce a numbing sensation in the mouth, but hopefully not enough to kill you. No, your nemesis is far more likely to be one of the innocuous egg sand-wiches often found as the middle of a set of three in a convenience-store chill cabinet. Particularly in Japan's swelteringly hot summer, there is no guarantee that such sandwiches were not packed half a day earlier, moved from factory to truck to store, left in sunlight and chilled once more in a fridge. If anything's going to take you out of action for a couple of days, it's one of those.

Despite an international ban on commercial whaling in force since 1982, Japanese whalers persist in engaging in 'lethal experiments' each year and then selling their catch on to restaurants. This has made Japan one of the few places in the world where you can try whale meat. The best place to find such contraband is in pop-up shops in Yokohama, but you can also find it shelved as **obaike** in some supermarkets. There is even a whale restaurant in Shinjuku. Unwilling to support such flagrant and cynical disregard of international law, I have never tried whale meat, so know nothing more about it.

Drink

For the most ancient taste of Japan, look to the dashi broth that forms the basis of so many Japanese soups and stews. It is made from bonito fish, boiled and then smoked into hard blocks that can last for years. This made it possible for ancient coast-dwellers to trade them inland, thereby forming one of the cornerstones of the prehistoric Japanese economy. The fish blocks ended up so hard that they were of little use for anything except as a very chewy jerky or a powdered base for soups. More modern soup bases, of course, use miso paste made from soy beans, dating merely from medieval times.

The tourist's most recurring encounter with actual Japanese drinks is liable to be in the form of the ubiquitous vending machines found on streets and in the lobbies of the more spartan hotels and hostels, dispensing both hot and cold drinks, including coffee in cans. Soft drinks can also be found in the equally widespread convenience stores. More seasoned Tokyo city walkers will soon develop a habit of ducking into such places on every other block in the summer, for both rehydration and a brief respite beneath the air conditioning.

Japanese tea is a palimpsest of foreign imports. The oldest and most traditional is **matcha**, deriving from the kind of tea drunk in China during the Tang dynasty, when cultural contacts were first established with the mainland. It comes as green powder and is an acquired taste, although I confess I can't get enough of it. It is oddly expensive abroad, so worth stocking up on if you like it, particularly if you want to also use it for its modern perversion, green tea ice cream, in which a spoonful of matcha powder is mixed into a bowl of plain vanilla, imparting a delightful colour and taste.

A more recent Chinese import, **ūron** (oolong) uses a part-roasted and fermented leaf, and hence results in a brown brew. Jasmine tea is also common, although the fact it is called **jazumin** when perfectly serviceable terms exist in both Chinese and Japanese immediately raises suspicions that its popularity only arose in the nineteenth century when it was brought in by the British.

When it comes to alcohol, unless you are alone and

have no choice, it is usual for companions to pour each other's drinks. Keep your tablemate's drink topped up to show kindness and social obligation. If you've had enough, then stop drinking and they won't be able to top you up – this is the origin of the common Japanese hand signal for 'enough', which is a hand held gently over a cup that does not require further filling. Although you will often be told that *kanpai* is Japanese for cheers, it literally means 'dry cup' and implies that you should drain your glasses. Say it sparingly, or make sure you are holding one of those sake cups that are barely larger than a thimble.

Shōchū (burned liquor) is cognate with the Korean *soju* and the Chinese *shaojiu* and appears to have entered Japan with Chinese sailors during the Nanban era. It's a potent grain-based 25%-alcohol firewater drunk neat or mixed, and for many years was thought of as something of a blue-collar booze or tramp's tipple. Ardent and successful marketing in the late twentieth century managed to persuade young women that it was a ladies' drink, particularly when served in the form of the Can Chū-Hi alcopops found in many vending machines – so much so that the author often elicits taunts and giggles when he drinks one.

The most famous Japanese drink, of course, is **sake** rice 'wine' – although, with a raw alcohol content of 18–20%, it is rather strong for wine. Sometimes it is diluted with water before bottling, leading to lower percentages being listed on the label. For hundreds of years, sake brewing remained a temple-based activity, likely reflecting that it, along with writing and Buddhism, had been introduced by Chinese monks in the medieval period. To this day, the term in Japanese for a sake brewer is *Tōji* (Mr Du), which derives from Du Kang, the legendary Chinese inventor of the process. Brewing became far more widespread with the introduction of modern technology in the Meiji period, leading to government initiatives that steered consumption away from home brews and towards businesses that could be more readily regulated and taxed. This included a ban on home brewing in 1904, but also public tasting competitions that encouraged sake to, well, taste of something and not strip the enamel off your teeth.

Sake can be served at room temperature, chilled or even warmed, although this latter version is a winter toddy best undertaken only with the cheaper varieties. A sake snob will be aghast if you try to warm up a more expensive brand. Do not be surprised if your pourer over-fills the cup to insane levels, perhaps even spilling into the *masu* saucer in which it stands. This is a sign of generosity – although if you try it, it is sure to be a sign that the foreigner can't pour properly.

The technology for beer was imported during the Meiji era. Kirin in Yokohama, Asahi in Ōsaka and Sapporo in, well, Sapporo. Yebisu beer was first brewed in Tokyo in 1890, deriving its name from a god of good fortune. Now a subsidiary of Sapporo, the brewery was moved out to Chiba in 1988, leading to the renovation of the former site into a park that bears its name, containing a shopping complex and the Museum of Yebisu Beer (see Gazetteer: Shibuya).

Japanese whisky distillers trained in Scotland during the Meiji era of modernisation and brought their know-how back to their homeland. If you're wondering why so many Japanese whisky brands are winning awards, it may be because they're reaping the investments of the 1980s Bubble era, when expensive, custom brands were left in barrels to mature, and are only now finding their way onto the market. If, however, that is true, then perhaps we are just about to experience a sudden slump in the quality of Japanese whisky, or at least its availability, as the 1990s barrels come online.

9

Travel Logistics

VISA-FREE ACCESS for up to 90 days applies to most tourists arriving in Japan from European or English-speaking countries. Citizens of certain other countries, including Malaysia, Serbia and Turkey, get the same treatment but only if they have a biometric passport. Visitors from Russia and the former Soviet Union, China and the Philippines must apply for visas in advance.

Tokyo is an easy place to get around. Signage and announcements are often in English as well as Japanese, and ever since the 1964 Olympics town planners have enthusiastically adopted universal icons rather than Japanese writing on such places as toilets and emergency exits. Travelling around Tokyo public transport is easy with a PASMO or Suica card – they are made by rival companies but work in the same way, being charged with cash and then tapped in and out. They work on all buses and trains within the Tokyo area (and within some other metropolises), except long-distance routes and airport shuttles, and can often be used as debit cards in convenience stores and at vending machines. If you are planning to travel outside Tokyo, do consider a Japan Rail Pass, which permits unlimited travel on Japan Rail networks for a set number of days. Although you can purchase one within Japan at certain major stations, it is advisable, both in terms of costs and logistics, to buy one from a travel agency before you arrive in Japan. A seven-day card will pay for itself easily with just a couple of return trips outside of town (to Kyōto, for example), a return trip from the airport and a few days shunting around the public transport system. It will even allow for a few tourist hacks, such as staying in Yokohama instead and getting the 18-minute bullet train into Tokyo each morning 'for free'. The Japan Rail Pass allows for free seat reservations, which can otherwise double the price of some tickets. Please note, however, that it does not work on private networks, nor on the Nozomi-class (super-express) bullet train.

If travelling around the rest of Japan, try to make use of the *takkyūbin* services, which transport luggage from hotel to hotel and save you the bother of carrying it yourself. You can even arrange to dump your cases at the airport and have them freighted straight to your hotel. The savings in not needing a taxi at either end can often make the service pay for itself, and it will make your trip much easier if you are not lugging a suitcase around stations and looking in vain for somewhere to stash it on a Japanese train.

When it comes to getting stuff home again, Japanese post offices are a dream come true. You can arrive with the articles you want to post and buy a *yūbin-hako* (posting box) to put them in, then use the materials on site to tape it shut and address it.

Because many Japanese cash machines in banks do not accept foreign credit cards or bank cards, your best bet is to use the ones in post offices or 7-Elevens, as well as Seven Bank machines that can be found in many department stores, railway stations, FamilyMarts and Lawson convenience stores. As for the money you put in your pocket, the 2004-series Japanese banknotes come in three denominations: 1,000, 5,000 and 10,000 yen. The crazy-haired guy on the 1,000-yen note is **Noguchi Hideyo** (1876–1928), a prominent medical researcher renowned in his lifetime for chasing down the origins of several diseases and infections. However, much of his research subsequently became outmoded or was disproven, which means that his greatest surviving achievements include the use of snake venom in serums, and identifying the causative agent of syphilis in partial paralysis – which is all very useful, but a strange reason to put him on a banknote. The 5,000-yen note bears the image of the novelist **Higuchi Ichiyō** (1872–1896), who died in her twenties having written a handful of highly regarded stories evocative of late-nineteenth-century Tokyo life. The 10,000-yen note has, since 1984, shown the stern face of **Fukuzawa Yukichi** (1835–1901), an author, entre-preneur and thinker instrumental in founding many important institutions of the Meiji era, and renowned for theorising about Japan's place in the modern world. He is, frankly, the only person with banknote status who really deserves it. I have no idea why the other two were selected over dozens of better-known and more influential figures from Japanese history.

10

Gazetteer

AS WITH ALL OTHER PUBLICATIONS in the Armchair Traveller series, this book offers a brief outline of some of the more interesting sites, with an emphasis on history and culture. But Tokyo is too large an entity, both in time and space, for any single guide to convey what it has to offer. A list such as this can only use the broadest possible strokes to delineate the areas of interest in any particular district, and to point the reader at the more recent alterations that may have eluded older books, such as the closure of the TEPCO Electric Power History Museum in 2011, and the relocation of the Tobacco & Salt Museum to new premises in a different district in 2015. The ever-spiralling prices of Tokyo real estate can lead to some sudden disappearances when someone realises they can, say, move an institution further afield, rebuild it on bigger premises and still have enough profit from the sale of the former location to buy themselves a condo in Vancouver. Considering that even the Tsukiji Fish Market moved out of Tsukiji in 2018, the Japan visitor is advised to double-check any planned itinerary or give in to the inevitable discovery of a half a dozen unexpected places that they weren't even looking for.

I tender my apologies in advance to readers who have taken to heart the more breathless comments of Japanese tourist guides and bristle with anger if I don't mention repeatedly how lovely a particular temple looks when there are cherry blossoms in the spring. While it is doubtless true in thousands of cases, it is often also a rather desperate attempt to find something to say about a place that is unremarkable for the other 50 weeks a year – or, even worse, entirely picturesque but unattended until it is pig-piled by hordes of tourists for a single springtime fortnight. Tour guides the world over like to talk things up, but there can be a frustrating performativity in Japanese marketing materials, which are often determined to follow a haiku-like template of seasonal keywords and synonyms for beauty. Strip them out, as I once did for an appalled group in the elevator at Kyōto Tower, and it amounts to: '*In spring, it looks nice / in summer, it also looks nice / but you won't believe how it looks in autumn... any guesses?*'

Similarly, I simply lack the space to mention every single temple and shrine. Tokyo has over 13,000 – more than any other place in Japan, although substantially fewer per head of population than more religious areas like Shiga or Fukui. I say this not to be deliberately difficult, but also to prevent the common sensation among foreign visitors of being 'templed out', forced to glumly trudge around yet another collection of religious buildings. Unless you are of Shintō or Buddhist faith, and the nuances of particular Goddess of Mercy or Shakyamuni statues are exciting to you, the locations mentioned in this Gazetteer should be more than enough for you; they have been selected for their importance in context to the history of Tokyo itself, as well as their presence in many visitors' recommended lists.

Most museums are liable to be closed on Mondays – or, if the Monday is a national holiday, open on the holiday and closed the day after. As a rule of thumb, double-check opening times for any place you plan on visiting on a Monday, and certainly don't do something stupid like sitting on a bullet train for three hours to see a place that happens to be closed. I've done that, so you don't have to.

Like most cities that grow organically and haphazardly, Tokyo lacks a grid system or carefully balanced zoning. Some may quibble with the organisational system here and complain that, say, the temple at Sengaku-ji is just as much part of Shinjuku as it is part of Minato. A lot of these places are shoved surprisingly close to one another.

Chichijima

An exception to the dense layout of Tokyo is Chichijima, an island which is 25 hours away by the Ogasawara Maru ferry from the Takeshiba docks in Minato ward. The ferry runs every three days in each direction, but travellers are advised to leave a little wiggle room on their itineraries in case rough weather slows it down – sometimes it might take a couple of extra hours to make port. A one-way ticket in a second-class cabin is 30,000 yen (£200). Modern travellers surgically attached to their phones are often caught off guard by the sudden loss of a signal once out of sight of land – don't bank on being able to check your email on the way.

Chichijima and Hahajima ('Father Island' and 'Mother Island') are the only inhabited islands in the Ogasawara archipelago, and tourists can travel by boat to go whale watching, scuba dive, explore the bird sanctuary and do similar activities in the 'Galapagos of the Orient', where local flora and fauna are unique enough for the Ogasawara Islands to have qualified for UNESCO World Heritage status in 2011. Chichijima is also home to a marine-life centre and the VERA radio telescope station.

Don't expect to be able to just pop over to Iwo Jima, which remains off limits to casual visitors. Trips there are exclusively in the hands of the company Military Historical Tours (www.miltours.com) and need to be booked far in advance. They tend to fly in from Guam, so are not really part of a 'Japanese' itinerary.

Chiyoda/Akihabara

The **Imperial Palace** is the most historically important site in the very centre of Tokyo. The innermost grounds are open to the public only once a year. It is possible to get on a twice-daily guided tour arranged by the Household Agency in the north-west grounds, but places are limited, and the tour is conducted in Japanese via loudhailer. The tour is heavily regimented, and there are no toilet breaks. You will also not be allowed in without recognised ID, so don't forget to bring your passport. If you do not speak Japanese, you will have to muddle through with an English phone app.

The **East Gardens** are closed on Mondays and Fridays, but otherwise can be entered – the regimented tour actually finishes here, bypassing any queues, in order to give you the feeling that you have actually been able to wander a little more freely. Remember, however, both to take a token from the security guards at the gate, and to hand it back when you leave so they know nobody is left behind after dark.

Across the road from the Imperial Palace is the **National Museum of Modern Art**. The central area of Tokyo also has a bunch of museums hidden away on upper floors, such as one on the sixth floor of the **Hotel New Ōtani**, and another, the **Idemitsu Museum of Arts**, on the ninth floor of the **Imperial Theatre** building.

The controversial **Yasukuni Shrine** is an incredible

experience for the Tokyo tourist, but often for all the wrong reasons. Linking practically every family in Japan through its list of 2 million deceased in the Book of Souls, it is a magnet for earnest worshippers, visitors and donors, while its museum presents a fascinating insight into the story that the Japanese tell themselves about the Second World War. It has such a connection to the old ways and the Japanese establishment that the incumbent abbot is a Mr Tokugawa. Provocative but also thought-provoking, it is a challenging sight. Entrance to the shrine itself is free, but the Yūshūkan museum will take an 800-yen entrance fee. Be sure to peruse the guest book, which often has some frank comments scrawled by scandalised foreign visitors, and the gift shop, which is a treasure trove of ideological horrors. In terms of bang for your buck, there is so much more to see here than at practically any other temple – but be warned that even stepping onto the grounds is a red rag to some, and the money you pay in admission goes to the upkeep of a venue that glorifies the architects of Pearl Harbor. In 2013, a Chinese arsonist went unpunished for attempting to set fire to it because South Korea refused to extradite him for trial in Japan. In 2014, Justin Bieber inadvertently tweeted some pictures of himself larking around in what to him was just another pretty temple, only to stir up a storm of angry protest from his Chinese and Korean fans. In 2015, an unidentified protestor let off a bomb in the toilets.

Less lively, at least most of the time, is the **Kanda Shrine**, which dates from the early Middle Ages, and where medieval residents would hold a careful parade to appease the spirit of their neighbour from hell, the demonic Masakado. It was originally close to Tokugawa Ieyasu's castle, leading the victorious Shōgun to co-opt the parade as a celebration of his own victory at Sekigahara, and for a long while the parade was the only opportunity for commoners to see inside the castle grounds, as part of it would purposefully wind through the outer keep to give the aristocrats an eyeful. The parade still happens on 15 May of every odd-numbered year, and crams the temple with celebrants and activity. The extant buildings, however, date from 1934, and feature lavish carvings from the sculptor Kitamura Seibō, who is better known for the Prayer for Peace statue in Hiroshima.

It is well attended even at other times; besides Masakado, two of its enshrined deities are gods of prosperity, and attract reverence from superstitious businessmen. In recent years, the Kanda Shrine has also embraced its proximity to the Akihabara shopping district and sells amulets that supposedly protect electronic products from harm. They make for quirky souvenirs and may even stop your crazy aunt from crashing the 'Windows machine' again.

If you prefer something quieter, the **Hie Shrine** is far more modest, except in June of even-numbered years, when it becomes the epicentre of the all-day Sannō Matsuri festival. This also dates from the days of Ieyasu, and now features celebrants dressed in ancient costume or attired as *karasu-tengu* (crow demons), carrying mikoshi shrines through the streets of the political district. The event is usually preceded for several days by sin-purging activities at the temple itself, and exhibits such as ikebana flower arrangements or tea tasting.

Akihabara itself is a shopping Mecca for electronics. Larger stores offer a duty-free waiver (bring your passport), but I confess that the prospect of a mere 8% discount usually leaves me cold. Unless you're looking for some kind of special device only available in Japan (a WordTank e-dictionary, for example), I question whether the saving is really worth it for a product that you can probably order online and have waiting for you at home. There are certainly not *huge* bargains to be had unless you are a bulk-buyer for a bank's IT department, although sometimes Akihabara's cutting-edge stores can offer something for the early adopter. But otherwise, Akihabara's original reputation is somewhat out of date, based on the breathless reports of 1980s tourists, before the days of online ordering and, even within Japan, of the rise of ubiquitous superstores like Bic Camera.

Akihabara is much more justifiably famed in recent years as an otaku paradise, pivoting away from electronics into media, merchandise and anything collectable. There is a veritable cornucopia of stuff for the anime or manga fan and bargains galore, since some of its stores favour obscurities, discontinued items and high-end second-hand goods. But if you're serious about shopping, be prepared to put in the hours and look to the skies. The ground-floor stores often have to charge higher prices to offset their rents. Climb the stairs to the smaller shops in the storeys above to stand a chance of really scoring some bargains. Female customers who baulk at the guy-pandering nature of it all might like to try the more lady-friendly shopping to be found on the Otome Road (see Gazetteer: Toshima/Ikebukuro).

The nearby **Jinbocho** area is famous for its second-hand bookstores, although these sell prose books – if you're looking for manga, Akihabara is where you want to be.

Chūō/Ginza

Literally on the other side of the tracks from Chiyoda is Chūō, formerly the site of the foreigners' concession after Tokyo was opened to outsiders. No evidence of this 1870s occupation remains today, quite possibly for the best, as nobody seems to have been all that impressed with it. Henry Faulds wrote in his *Nine Years in Nipon* of the misery of his 'barrack-like wooden building... the chief objection to which was a plague of frogs. They were "fat and full of sap", and seemed never to be happy unless when getting under one's feet. At night they keep the sour reedy swamp which was honoured with the title of "compound" vocal with their hoarse paeans'.

In more recent times, it famously became the home of the **Tsukiji Fish Market**, although its long-postponed relocation to Toyosu finally happened in 2018. You can no longer wander around gawking at the produce – it's strictly business, although you can attend the attached shops and restaurant as a punter. If you are really serious about seeing the inside, then guided tours are likely to still be available in the new location, coupled with a sushi-making workshop.

Remodelled in 1872 after a fire, **Ginza** ('Silver Mint') became the home to Japan's first swanky department stores – it remains the most expensive square on the Japanese Monopoly board, which makes Sony's decision to stick a pop-up park in the middle of it all the more attention grabbing. High-end branded goods are still a thing here, although a weekend initiative to attract more casual consumers has led to the 'Pedestrian Paradise' – government tourist-speak for the road being closed to traffic from noon till dusk every Saturday and Sunday, creating a car-free promenade complete with capering mimes, dancers, puppeteers and hawkers. As in many other countries, the real estate is so expensive here that many brands merely site stores here as a form of advertising, with no hope of monetising through sales. This means in turn that many 'flagship stores', designed to show off next year's models or fashions, can give the dedicated shopper a glimpse of tomorrow, and occasionally play host to art galleries or exhibitions just to get people talking.

Eastern Suburbs

Parts of eastern Tokyo are a 'zero metre' zone, effectively below sea level and hence doubly prone to flooding in the event of a seawall breach or similar natural emergency. This only intensifies the already-prolific urban flood-prevention measures in the area, with tiny streams walled off behind massive berms and inland floodgates. Alex Kerr, in *Dogs and Demons*, suggests this is overkill: a series of white-elephant boondoggles designed to funnel cash into the cement and construction industry – but sometimes it might well not be.

The east of the city is home to two celebrations of the city's past. The bizarrely shaped **Edo-Tokyo Museum** (technically in Sumida) is designed to resemble an old warehouse, elevated off the ground with the exhibits themselves built into the 'attic'. It offers an informative introduction to the samurai-era city and may help put the city's transformations in perspective for the new visitor. Its most chilling exhibit is an animated display that reinflicts the firebombings of 1945 on Tokyo. Outside there is a bizarre statue of Ieyasu, the first Tokugawa Shōgun, brandishing a hawk and standing on a pillar that is itself on top of a gormless-looking tortoise. This is plainly an attempt to emulate the mythological *bixi* beasts that bear stone tablets in Chinese temples, but Ieyasu looks like a drunken student doing it for a bet. For a more ground-level experience, the **Fukagawa Edo Museum** recreates an entire nineteenth-century Tokyo street, warts and all, and is similarly evocative in illustrating how it must have felt to live in those times.

The **Shibamata** district is home to the lively **Taishakuten** temple, but is best known among the Japanese as the location for many of the 48 instalments of the movie series *Otoko ga Tsurai yo* (*It's Tough to be a Man*). Its star, Atsumi Kiyoshi (1928–96) played the itinerant peddler

Tora-san, a kindly buffer with a battered suitcase, whose adventures inevitably involve running into an eligible bachelorette (a 'Madonna' in movie parlance) somewhere in Japan, re-encountering her back on his Shibamata home turf, and helping her out with a problem that leaves him eternally friend-zoned and heartbroken. Although Tora-san was a Japanese cultural icon that failed to attract widespread foreign notice, his melancholy striving for love and recognition touched a chord with men of Atsumi's generation, and Shibamata itself has become a shrine to the movies' locations, events and characters. Tora-san himself would be baffled and a little disturbed to see his calculatedly nondescript and average hometown turned into a living museum to a media commodity. No doubt he would then get tearful because his hometown has noticed his myriad good deeds.

Meguro

This unassuming district derives its name from the deity that guards the entrance to the **Ryūsen-ji** ('Dragon Springs Temple'), the *me-guro* (black-eyed) King of Wisdom. The temple itself is pleasantly secluded, and decorated throughout with Buddhist and dragon motifs. Its sites of interest include **Takasue-no-matsu**, a tree given special status by Iemitsu, the third Tokugawa Shōgun, because his pet falcon, believed lost, was found sitting in it.

Other spots of likely tourist interest include the **Meguro Museum of Art**, which specialises in modern Japanese works, and the **Museum of Parasitology**, if you want to see a really long tapeworm. Among several parks and picnic-worthy temple grounds, the area also boasts the **Institute for Nature Study**, which doubles as a nature reserve and a park for old people at a loose end, since pensioners get in free, as do kids.

Minato

Literally the 'Harbour' district, Minato incorporates several sub-districts liable to turn up on the itineraries of tourists or visitors on business. Its Shiba area was once the religious centre of Tokyo, a citadel of wealthy temples that serviced the needs of the Tokugawa Shōgunate. The **Maruyama Keyhole Tomb** still survives as a wooded hill within the park, and the presence of this large tomb for an unknown Dark Age ruler indicates that the area was likely first a graveyard. But as a 'Shōgunal' site it became rich pickings for the Shōgun's enemies when he was overthrown in the Meiji Restoration. The entire district was downgraded, plundered and requisitioned in a series of purges in the late nineteenth century, while the Second World War air raids destroyed most of the remaining shrines and tombs. The southern reaches were written off as one of Tokyo's first industrial zones, becoming home to such companies as Tōkyō Shiba-ura Denki (Tokyo Inner Shiba Electronics), better known today by its abbreviation: Toshiba.

Much of the area turned into parkland, which was itself slowly repurposed through a series of private enclosures, such as a golf course that shut out non-players, and well-meaning insult was added to injury when the area was repurposed yet again as the site for Tokyo Tower. No longer a broadcast antenna, and far from being the best vantage point from which to look down upon the city, the tower has become a rather pointless, vestigial inclusion on organised tours, and frankly is only of interest to *Godzilla* fans who want to see the big stripy Eiffel Tower thing that so regularly gets trashed in all the movies. There have been some attempts to augment the tourist experience with a wax museum and a hall of mirrors, but even these ideas seem peculiarly old fashioned. On a note of desperation, it is now home to an exhibition of life-sized figures from the *One Piece* anime and manga franchise. It does, however, permit a bird's-eye view of one of the most striking edifices in modern Tokyo, the **Shakaden** temple, headquarters of the Reiyūkai religious organisation, which looks like a Star Destroyer that has landed in the middle of the city. It legendarily contains a reservoir that holds 400 tonnes of drinking water – considering that an estimated 70% of Tokyo's water mains are liable to collapse in the event of an earthquake, this might one day become the most important building in the city.

A trip to Tokyo Tower will put you close to two historically interesting temples, the **Sengaku-ji** ('Spring Hill Temple'), site of the tomb of the wronged Lord Asano, famously avenged by his 47 Rōnin henchmen. It was here that the masterless samurai came after they had killed his enemy, leaving the man's head on his grave before awaiting the Shōgun's assuredly rough justice. The henchmen, too, were buried here after their mass suicide, making the temple a popular spot on the domestic Japanese tourist trail. Even closer at hand is the **Zōjō-ji** ('Monk Upper Temple'), previously renowned as the last resting place of six Tokugawa Shōguns, but more appreciated today as being one of the best places to get an unrestricted ground-level view of Tokyo Tower. Consequently, you might find that your attempts to catch a Godzilla-style selfie interfere with a bunch of news camera crews trying to get a nice background.

Shinbashi ('New Bridge') was once the site of the first modern railway station in the city, part of which has been preserved as a 'museum' that is really an excuse for a railway-themed food court. The nearby Caretta Shiodome mall, however, is host to the **Ad Museum**, 'the only museum of advertising in Japan'. Run by the Dentsū corporation, the site is a fascinating introduction to Japan's world-beating marketing savvy, and contains a particularly interesting section on wartime propaganda. Go for that, and for the entreating brand statement, which seems to ignore many of the lessons of the advertising world and witters on about 'laughter and tears: astonishment and empathy', before feebly protesting: 'Advertising is fun!'

Roppongi ('Six Trees') originally derived its name from half a dozen samurai landowners who all had the word *–ki* (tree) in their surname. It was the site of army accommodation in the early modern era, and hence was swiftly overrun during the Occupation by foreign soldiers and embassies. Businesses catering to outsiders soon sprang up and endured long after the soldiers had gone, turning the area into a foreigner-friendly nightlife and shopping spot. This has allowed it to endure as a shopping and entertainment district. The area's most prominent landmark is the wavy-fronted **National Art Center** as well as the **Mori Tower** that soars above the Roppongi Hills development. As ever, look for museums squirrelled above your head, like the **Suntory Museum of Art**, tucked away on the third floor of Tokyo Midtown, and the **Mori Art Museum** which sprawls across the 52nd and 53rd floors of the Mori Tower. If you want a view of the city, then the **Tokyo City View** on its roof does exactly what it says on the tin, although its rooftop zone is closed during extreme weather. It even gives you a good view of Tokyo Tower, which only renders the latter even more redundant.

Odaiba, the former location of six gun batteries built in 1853 in vague hope of holding off Commodore Perry's Black Ships on their next visit, is now home to **Tokyo Big Sight**, Japan's largest exhibition centre. Some of the nearby attractions seem designed to distract listless businessmen on a junket, such as the **Toyota Mega Web** concept-car showroom, the **Museum of Maritime Science** and the **Mirai-kan** ('Future Pavilion'), a museum of science and technology.

Odaiba's tourist office has done everything it can to promote the area as the ideal place for dates and canoodling, and it plays to this image with a Ferris wheel, a beachfront promenade and a Venice-themed shopping mall, because everybody loves being shoved around in a gondola. Perhaps this is just my jaded cynicism talking, but I can't help but feel that a lot of the Odaiba attractions are more intent than usual on fleecing the passing traffic, and capitalising on the likelihood that at least one member of each couple will be trying to impress the other. There is a certain carnival atmosphere about the whole district, bringing with it a general attitude of *'Hey, what's another 10,000 yen? You only live once!'* Nowhere is this more obvious than the **Partire Tokyo Bay Wedding Village**, which offers to micromanage every aspect of your nuptials, complete with a fake foreign priest and wedding photography in a fake European town. The samurai-era-themed **Oedo-Onsen Monogatari** is a spa and shopping mall that asks patrons to hand over their credit card details and log all payments on an all-too-easily-triggered digital bracelet. To add insult to injury, the small print includes a late surcharge for staying in the spa after hours, even if you've booked a hotel there! There are many shopping malls, although you may find that prices are slightly higher than in the city proper, once again to reflect the likelihood that many of the shoppers will be ducking in for last-minute gifts as they rush home from a conference. Don't get me wrong; there's a lot of fun to be had in Odaiba – but watch your wallet.

Northern Suburbs

The radish and potato farms of Kita, Itabashi and Nerima were repurposed as real estate in the 1950s and 1960s, as the expanding rail and road networks favoured market gardens further afield. They hence became the centres of rising industries in the mid-twentieth century. Nerima in particular became the home of the Tōei Company film studio and its newly acquired animation wing in 1956. By the 1960s, Japan's booming animation business made Nerima and nearby Suginami prime sites for Tōei's numerous subcontracting studios, as well as their rivals. As a consequence of the proximity of the studios, many incidental locations in famous anime – parks, coffee shops, shopping malls – turn out to be real places in Nerima, snapped or sketched by passing animators and turned into scenes, making the area a popular 'holy land' destination for anime fans. In a triumph of recursion, you can find some fans tracing the routes of the old city trams, in homage to the two anime characters who do the same in Hara Keiichi's 2010 film *Colorful*, itself a nod to the forgotten locations of the animation studios that used to be situated along that line.

The area remains something of a media hub, and is home to several academic institutions churning out new artists and producers. The **Suginami Animation Museum** is run by former animators, and the centre of Nerima itself is scattered with bronze statues of twentieth-century cartoon characters.

The **Akasui-mon** ('Redwater Gate') no longer operates as one of the emergency floodgates that protects downstream Tokyo from rushing snowmelt or rain run-off, but has been left intact as the centrepiece of a local park.

The **Ōtori** ('Great Bird') Shrine in Nerima liked to bill itself as the 'Western Market' in Tokugawa times, and is still the site of a November festival. Owing to a regrettable translation slip on the part of a forgotten official or shrine maiden, this is now widely known as the **Cock Market**. You can still buy ceremonial bamboo *kumade* (bear claw) rakes there, in order to 'rake in' the money in the year to come.

Shibuya

The former site of the castle of the 'Bitter Valley' family, Shibuya enjoyed a brief reputation in the 1990s as 'Bit Valley', home of many a high-tech company. But most of its modern-day reputation and tourism value has sprung from its long-term usage as a railway hub. It was the place where Yokohama travellers could enter Tokyo and join the local transport network, and is still one of the stops for the Narita Express that connects Tokyo to the outside world. One of its station exits has been renamed after its most famous resident, **Hachikō** the faithful hound (see Chapter 5), who waited here for a master who would never return, and who is now commemorated with a statue. He's close to the **scramble crossing**, a five-way zebra crossing beneath a giant TV screen – a combination that seems to have become a popular choice among film-makers seeking to represent Japanese modernity. The best view of the crossing is from the massive Starbucks that looks down on it from the Tsutaya building.

The modern skyscrapers here obscure much of the winding dales and dead-end valleys that make navigating this part of town such a maze. The scholar and author Paul Waley, with evident frustration, describes it having all the regularity of 'the puckered hems of a badly sewn dress'. In an era where people are apt to navigate by a map on a cell phone, many an apparent shortcut turns out to be a blocked route or an unnecessary climb up a previously unknown slope.

Shibuya is primarily a self-consciously trendy fashion and shopping district, although the fact that each shopping mall is trying to compete for customer traffic with every other one has led to a ridiculously high count of 'museums' in the area. Last time I looked, there were almost 70, including a surfeit of art galleries, which a small book such as this lacks the space to chronicle in detail. Many of these attractions are designed as bait for Japanese shoppers, and hence are often lacking in resources for foreign visitors. The **NHK Studio Park**, for example, offers a plethora of children's play experiences, although many of its mascots and photo ops will mean nothing to those who do not watch the NHK TV channel. A notable exception is the **Samurai Museum**, which offers informative guided tours in both English and Japanese (and has a quality gift shop). Only a few others really stick out – in particular the **Ota Memorial Museum of Art**, which has a wonderful collection of Japanese woodblock prints, and the **Yamatane Museum of Art**, which similarly favours local artists. It's worth a visit not only for its artwork, but for the selection in the gift shop, which is also better than most.

The **Kawamoto Kihachirō Doll Museum**, on the eighth floor of the Shibuya Hikarie mall, celebrates the life and art of a man popularly known for the puppets he made for numerous kids' TV shows, but also for the arthouse reputation he gained from his stop-motion films. The **Bunka Gakuen Costume Museum**, a smartly curated historical view of world fashions, switches its exhibits four times a year, meaning that whatever you think you saw there last will be replaced whenever you go again. **Espace Louis Vuitton** is a modern art gallery designed to impart some cultural cachet to a retail outlet, but it can be famously at the cutting edge – it was once the place to see exclusive anime art pieces, and is sure to have something similarly off the wall if you can make it to the seventh floor without buying a handbag. For the visitor who wants to see more of truly ancient Japan, the permanent collection at the **Kokugakuin University Museum** has many prehistoric artefacts nestled in its shadowy halls.

The 42nd-floor **Tōgō Memorial Museum** (see Chapter 6) is not, as one might first expect, a celebration of the 'Japanese Nelson', Admiral Tōgō, but the artist Tōgō Seiji, and is home to the famous Van Gogh *Sunflowers* that made international headlines at the height of the Bubble years. The context of the painting's acquisition, and what it meant for Japan, is arguably more of a tourist magnet than the painting itself.

The **Museum of Yebisu Beer** offers tours every 20 minutes that end with beer-tasting sessions, but the tours are in Japanese only. Non-linguists are better off regarding it as a gastropub with some beer-related exhibits, and should guide themselves using the English-language signage. Tokens to exchange for samples can be bought in the tasting area. The museum is in **Yebisu Garden Place**, which was repurposed from the site of the former brewery. The same site is home to the **Tokyo Metropolitan Museum of Photography**. Note that 'Yebisu' is merely an old-fashioned pronunciation of Ebisu, the name of the station one stop south of Shibuya. You're not going mad – the beer brand still uses the old lettering, but not the old pronunciation.

The **TEPCO Electric Power Historical Museum** was formerly a fun hands-on science experience for kids, although it has been shuttered since 2011, when TEPCO's public reputation took a nosedive in the wake of the Fukushima nuclear accident. 'We repeatedly apologise,' pleads the museum's website, suggesting that the location remains a ghoulish photo opportunity for visitors for whom the act of not getting in is itself a thing worth documenting.

Harajuku, the 'Plain Fort' or possibly the 'Flat Dorms', was an area of level ground on the outskirts of the old town that never got properly developed as farmland because the crop yields were poor. It hence remained open ground for longer than usual, and was used for billeting soldiers both in the Tokugawa period and the Occupation. When the old US dorms were cleared out, it was remodelled first as the Olympic stadium, and then as **Yoyogi Park**. Yoyogi Park and the shopping streets that encircle it have long been a place to observe the self-consciously performative antics of various youth tribes. You'll find them here on a Sunday: rockabillies, Para-Para girls, Gothic Lolitas, body-poppers, hipsters and rockers, all staking out a little patch of ground and posing for passers-by, while secretly hoping to be discovered by a fashion magazine or a music scout. The police occasionally move them along, but everybody seems to understand that they and the hawkers that accrete around them are part of the attraction of the area.

The grounds of the park segue into a forest that contains the **Meiji Shrine**, a temple to the deified spirit of Japan's Meiji Emperor, dedicated in 1920 but destroyed during the war – his actual tomb is down in Kyōto. Rebuilt through public subscription, the new site was a matter of such national pride for the Japanese that the local district and train station was renamed for it. Although many addresses still appear to be in 'Harajuku', the area and the former East Harajuku station nearby are officially known as **Jingū-mae** – 'in front of the shrine'.

The railway line and a couple of blocks of buildings cut between the shrine proper and its outer grounds, which amount to two more parks, including the 1964 Olympic stadium. As you walk between the two green areas, you can engineer a visit to the **Tōgō Shrine**, dedicated to Admiral Tōgō Heihachirō – do not confuse this, as a surprising number of Instagrammers seem to do, with the unrelated Tōgō art museum elsewhere in Shibuya, or with General Tōjō, the convicted war criminal. Admiral Tōgō was the hero of Meiji Japan's expansionist era, most notoriously for defeating the Russians in the 1905 Battle of Tsūshima. He died in 1936, hence avoiding any Second World War associations that might have been attached to any more recent military figures, although this shrine was built in 1940 by those very same militarists, hoping to bask a little in his glory. Today it hosts a museum and shop dedicated to Tōgō matters, but although older guidebooks may tell you that it is the site of a flea-and-antique market, it no longer appears to be. His battle flag, which spent much of the twentieth century in the possession of the British college where he studied, was returned to Japan in 2005 and can be seen here. It is the Z flag, an international maritime signal flag which in Japan means 'The fate of the Empire depends on this battle. Let each man do his utmost.' Unfortunately for the author of a Tōgō biography who used to wear one on his lapel in London, the same signal means 'I need a tug' to British sailors.

Shinagawa

Ōmori Shell Mounds Ruins Garden marks the location where Edward S. Morse set about a small hill with a trowel, inadvertently marking the beginning of Japanese archaeology and taking the first steps into documenting and chronicling the Japanese past. There's a bronze bust of Morse in the grounds, along with samples from the middens themselves. Some of the artefacts recovered from the mounds by Morse and by his successors are kept at the **Shinagawa Historical Museum**, a short walk to the north.

Shinjuku

Shinjuku seems to have become half-heartedly aware in recent years that historically it doesn't have a whole lot going for it. So much of its reputation is founded on shopping or ephemeral cultural attractions – like the pop-up karaoke theme bars that come and go too swiftly to be recognised in a history book, or the love hotels and strip clubs of Kabukichō, where people frankly make their own entertainment. Kabukichō, in particular, has become oddly embraced for its sin-city chic, particularly since the release of Ringo Shiina's song *Queen of Kabukichō*, the hard-luck tale of a prostitute abandoned by her mother at fifteen. 'The only thing I can sell is myself,' sing enthusiastic office-lady karaoke-goers with a frisson of naughtiness. 'If you come out of the east gate of Shinjuku station, you can see my territory.' Patrick Macias has suggested that the popularity of the song has less to do with the intimations of sex for sale, and more with the singer's downtrodden status, something with which many average Japanese strongly identified after the Bubble burst and the economy slumped.

The area is infamous for its hostess clubs, where female companions will gasp with excitement at everything you say and do, for as long as you are paying for their drinks, and its host clubs, where the womenfolk of Japan will pay handsome metrosexuals to pretend to like them, in some form of roundabout payback. The hostesses from the former are often said to be the best customers of the latter.

As a filming location in central Tokyo, however, Shinjuku proper has gained a few 'holy land' photo opportunities, including the twin towers of the **Metropolitan Government Offices**, home of the Japanese tax administration and, coincidentally, often the subject of wilful destruction in Japanese monster movies. There are free observation galleries on the 45th floors that offer views of the city not unlike that from the much-touted Tokyo Tower, the upper observation gallery of which is only 6 metres higher. A life-sized **Godzilla head** looms out between two of the buildings in Kabukichō, not far from the Tōhō Cinemas complex owned by the studio that birthed him. Impress your movie-nerd friends by observing that it is a life-sized, lifelike representation of Godzilla as seen in 1992's *Godzilla vs. Mothra*, not any of the redesigned looks from more recent movies.

The Shin-Okubo sub-district is also known as **Korea Town**, and has long been an enclave of Japan's ethnic Korean community. That might have once been likely to associate it with the wheeler-dealers of Kabukichō, but the surge of interest in K-pop and Korean culture within Japan has turned it into more of an addendum to Shinjuku, a self-styled arbiter of youth-culture cool. Recently, Shin-Okubo has suffered a little as the blush comes off the Korean rose – Japan's increasingly right-wing foreign policy and ongoing sabre-rattling over who owns the island of Dokdo has made a trip to Korea Town for kimchi, Innisfree cosmetics and boy-band posters less of a thing for modern Japanese. The Korean identity, which was once vibrant and obvious, has faded a little, and some of the shops have found new owners. One part of it has gained the new nickname *Islam Yokochō* (**Islam Alley**), as it caters to more newly arrived immigrants from western China and the Middle East.

Just adjacent to Shinjuku is Nakano ward, notable for the otaku-friendly Broadway Arcade north of the station. However, note that this pop-culture shoppers' paradise runs on the second floor, above ground level, and that the shopkeepers are night owls who tend to not open their doors until relatively late in the morning. Of greater relevance to the historian are the many statues of dogs that litter the area near the front gate of Nakano City Hall – it was here that Tokugawa Tsunayoshi, the 'Dog Shōgun', established a kennel that once cared for 10,000 strays.

Sumida

Relocated in 2015 from its former location in Shinagawa, the **Tobacco & Salt Museum** is a true oddity, dedicated to two commodities that were a government monopoly in the samurai era. The story of how an obscure South American narcotic leaf not only migrated to Japan, but somehow flourished and became an integral part of Japanese life during the centuries of isolation is strangely fascinating – not only for the smoker, but for the antique-shop browser wondering how the strange pouches, pipes and knick-knacks they have seen functioned in the old days. Salt, too, is one of those basic commodities that might seem dull, but was an integral part of old-time commerce and culture.

The **Japanese Sword Museum** also moved here to the riverside Kyū-Yasuda Garden from Shibuya in 2018. It was well worth a visit in its former location and presumably still is, although the new three-floor site still only has a single floor of actual exhibits. The rest of the space is taken up with a lecture hall, café and reading room, emphasising its role as not only a place for researchers, but a venue for hire, planning to monetise in other ways beyond simply showing people swords.

Toshima/Ikebukuro

A concentration of temples can be found in this ward, including the **Honmyō-ji**, where an attempt to exorcise a haunted kimono led to the cataclysmic city-wide Meireki Fire (see Chapter 3). The **Kōgan-ji** is renowned for two statues in particular – one said to heal sick children, and another that grants a peaceful death that does not trouble one's family. There are also some famous burials – Lafcadio Hearn, the mythologist of nineteenth-century Japan, is buried in the **Zōshigaya Cemetery**, and the vengeful Oiwa, the inspiration for many a creepy stalker in Japanese drama, is supposedly interred at the **Myōkō-ji**. Her grave is a popular place for actors to pay their respects – ever superstitious, many refuse to put on a show that mentions her without first praying before her tomb.

Ikebukuro ('Pond Bag' or, less literally, 'The Wetlands') was a low-lying area of marshes and lakes in the samurai era, site of the **Gokoku-ji** ('Country-Protecting Temple') founded by the dog-loving Shōgun Tokugawa Tsunayoshi. The temple is still standing today – remarkably, since most other buildings in Tokyo were destroyed in the Second World War. Brixton-born Josiah Conder, the architect of many of the great buildings of Japan's modernisation era, is buried in the cemetery here.

This area began to flourish during the Meiji period, particularly after the peculiarities of Tokyo geography required a railway junction station in the area to streamline the passage of several lines in and out of the city. The drained marshes became sites for cheap housing, and the area has retained a slightly cosmopolitan, bohemian feel to match the artistic types that initially flocked there. It is still the home, every April, to the New Year festival of Tokyo's Bangladeshi community. An art installation in a park on the west side of the station, resembling some prison doors on a family outing, is the **Tokyo Shaheed Minar**, a copy of a monument in Dhaka to Bangladesh's war of liberation. It is supposed to represent a mother and her fallen sons.

The east exit of the station is home to a statue of an *ike-fukurō* (pond-owl) a mascot for the area who derives his name from a chance pun. Owls have hence become something of a thing in Ikebukuro, and can be found adorning public spaces. There is even, so help me, an owl café. It seems oddly cruel to take light-sensitive, nocturnal wild predators and force them to be awake during the day in order to soothe troubled human breasts, but it is not the weirdest thing you will see in Tokyo.

The area north of Ikebukuro station is home to a small and little-discussed Tokyo **Chinatown**, which sprang up haphazardly among the immigrant population during the 1990s. Unlike Yokohama's Chinatown, which is authentically old but often feels more like a tourist trap, this is a genuine working district serving the Chinese population, to which the Japanese are permitted access somewhat grudgingly. Four entrance points are now graced with Chinese gates to make it feel like more of a reality. It's a good place to find real Chinese food.

One street in Ikebukuro has developed a reputation for selling pop-culture goodies with a special emphasis on female consumers. The **Otome Road** ('Maiden Road') bills itself as an antidote to the testosterone-heavy Boys' Club of the marketplaces of Akihabara.

The **Ancient Orient Museum** was founded in 1978, and is dedicated to all points west of Japan as far as Turkey, and often mounts fascinating exhibitions on subjects such as prehistoric Central Asia or Chinese antiquities.

Taito/Ueno

There was a time when the Asakusa district was the very hub of Tokyo life, stretching from around the time of the arrival of the Black Ships to the end of the Second World War. Part of the charm of the Taito area lies in how much of it *hasn't* changed – if you're very lucky, you can turn a corner from an anonymous twenty-first-century street and find yourself in a 1930s residential area, with wooden houses seemingly untouched by the wartime firebombs. Time, too, can take its toll, and many run-down areas have been redeveloped, or at least preserved for other purposes. A Meiji-era sake brewery in the area has been preserved as the **Shitamachi Museum Annex**, and is of particular interest to students of booze.

The main building of the **Shitamachi Museum** outlining the history of Tokyo's Low City area can be found in Ueno Park, which is also home to **Tokyo Zoo**, the multiple buildings of the **Tokyo National Museum**, the **National Museum of Nature and Science** and the **National Museum of Western Art**. Those alone should keep you busy for a few days. Watch your step around the **Shinobazu Pond**, site of the great bloodletting at the Battle of Ueno – this is also where the venerable Japanologist and Tokyo expert Edward Seidensticker slipped and bashed his head in 2007, never emerging from the subsequent coma.

A little to the north of Ueno Park, there is an unremarkable square of land roughly seven city blocks on each side, which labours under the name of Senzoku 4-chōme. Its very everydayness is something of a tourist attraction for the author, since this is the area that was once the fabled **Yoshiwara** brothel quarter, relocated here in 1656 to what was then the outskirts of the city. Largely burned down in 1913, and annihilated by the 1923 earthquake, the area has been so thoroughly built and rebuilt that there are only a couple of unobtrusive signs marking, for example, the former site of the **Great Yoshiwara Gate**, and a small park that keeps the Yoshiwara name. The only real indicator of what was once here is a larger concentration than usual of sex shops and girlie bars, but it's really not a patch on the area's glory days. Nor would anyone really want it to be.

Asakusa is also the upriver terminus for the **Tokyo Water Bus**, which runs down the Sumida River to Odaiba and back, or the Mizube Line, which runs between the Hama Rikyū Gardens and Asakusa, via Odaiba. Journeys take between 35 minutes and two hours, depending on the boat, the route and whether or not you are taking a more sedate lunch or dinner passage. It's a good way to see the city from the water, although some of the passages seem a little fast, designed more as actual bus services than as opportunities to admire the view.

Western Suburbs

Tokyo keeps on going until it turns into other cities – sit on the train for long enough and the city turns into Saitama ('the Land over the Tama River') or Yokohama ('Beachside'). The city just keeps on going; there's no Green Belt to speak of... and suddenly you're passing Mount Fuji and halfway to Nagoya. Mount Fuji seems to be the default limit for 'Tokyo-based' tours, which will take you for a bullet-train day trip encapsulating the lower slopes of the mountain and the lakeside resort of Hakone. At that point, however, you are crossing the border of a book about Tokyo.

There's not a lot for the foreign tourist to see in the suburb that actually bears the name Nishitōkyō ('Western Tokyo'), nor in its neighbouring areas of Musashino, which lent its name to the prehistoric tableland and the medieval province, or Kichiōji ('Auspicious Temple'). Koganei ('Little Gold Well') is home to the **Tatemono-en**, the Edo-Tokyo Museum's open-air architectural museum.

The Tama River valley is of vital archaeological importance, partly because of its Dark Age society, but also because it was built up in the late twentieth century, when the Japanese had a newfound respect for salvage archaeology and newfound money to afford it. The area's transformation from wooded hills to a jumble of storm drains and housing estates – much mourned in several Studio Ghibli films, particularly Takahata Isao's *Pom Poko* (1994) – was hence accompanied by a greater degree of preservation than had previously been afforded to more central areas. It's here that you'll find **Todoroki Gorge** and the ruins in **Tamagawa Nogemachi Park** (see Chapter 1). The Tama Hills are home to **Nihon Minka-en**, an outdoor museum of ancient Japanese farmhouses and technologies set within Ikuta Ryokuchi Park, as well as the **Studio Ghibli Museum** in Mitaka, which carefully manages the legacy of the great animation studio. The latter is a masterpiece of child-friendly design, arranged so that you are always wandering but never lost, and with wonderful little touches like the baubles at a toddler's-eye level on the staircase. Admission is capped daily and by timed entry booked at least three days in advance, but if you are there on a slow day, you can try to cheat the system by 'booking' your ticket at the Lawson convenience store near the entrance. This is, however, technically against the rules and not recommended – Studio Ghibli is such a draw for local visitors that 'slow days' are few and far between.

Tokyo has over 900 railway stations, every one of them the nexus of a place that was once a township or temple, every one scattered with shrines and cul-de-sacs of historical interest, that little noodle shop you can't resist, and the odd little park with a bust at the entrance of some minor samurai reformer. This book, by necessity, can only scratch the surface of Tokyo's historical existence. Your experience, of your Tokyo, can only begin when you step out of the door and start to walk.

Chronology of Major Events

TOKYO'S MODERN HISTORY spans the reigns of just four Emperors – Meiji (1868–1912), Taishō (1912–1925), Shōwa (1926–1989) and Heisei (1989–2019). It's worth knowing their names, because much signage in the capital assumes you already do, and something can be airily described as 'Meiji-era' with little context.

It's Meiji and Shōwa who dominate – Taishō, son of the former and father of the latter, presided over a brief interregnum in which the main Tokyo events were the inauguration of the shrine to his father's memory, and the earthquake that levelled the city. Mutsuhito, the Meiji Emperor, is remembered for the transformative Meiji Restoration that saw him enthroned as an ultra-modern monarch, ready to sweep away the samurai era. He saw in the great public works and early brick buildings that evoke nineteenth-century Japan for the modern tourist. Meiji's grandson, the Shōwa Emperor, Hirohito, witnessed much of the rest of the twentieth century – the rebuilding of Tokyo after the earthquake and the Second World War, its helter-skelter remodelling for the 1964 Olympics and later the 1980s boom economy.

Meiji's great-grandson Akihito, the Heisei Emperor, has also presided over a period featuring much change, but devoid of much of the flash and bombast, stuck instead in an austerity era of smaller-scale development and a few landmark projects like the Rainbow Bridge.

He is bowing out, by abdication, in 2019 – just ahead of Tokyo's second hosting of the Olympic Games in 2020, leaving his own son, Naruhito, to inaugurate a new era.

628	Asakusa Kannon temple (Sensō-ji) is founded
646	Musashi province is established
808	Ryūsen-ji temple is founded
939	Masakado's revolt
940	Masakado is killed and his head brought to Kyōto
1186	Edo Shigenaga founds the Keigen-ji temple in Kitami
1457	Ōta Dōkan builds Edo Castle
1486	Ōta Dōkan dies; Edo Castle is abandoned
1590	Edo becomes the headquarters for Tokugawa Ieyasu
1598	Ieyasu unifies state coinage by establishing a *ginza* (silver mint)
1593	Ogasawara Sadayori discovers the islands that now take his name
1603	Ieyasu becomes the first Tokugawa Shōgun; construction of the *Nihonbashi* ('Japan Bridge')
1617	Opening of the Yoshiwara pleasure quarter
1634	Construction work on Edo Castle pushes several shrines and temples to relocate to Yotsuya
1635	Iemitsu, the third Tokugawa Shōgun, initiates the *sankin kōtai* policy that mandates alternating attendance in Edo for all feudal lords
1635–39	The Sakoku Edicts highly limit foreign contacts, particularly with Europeans
1654	Completion of Tamagawa Aqueduct

1657	Meireki Fire kills 100,000 and burns down most of the city; Yotsuya is spared, and consequently flourishes
	Area east of the Sumida River begins to grow
1670	Japanese sailors rediscover the Ogasawara Islands, later part of Tokyo Municipality
1673	Opening of the Echigoya kimono shop, which would eventually become the Mitsukoshi department store
1685	Edo is plagued by packs of dogs after Tsunayoshi, the fifth Shōgun, proclaims the Laws on Compassion for All Living Things
1707	Eruption of Mount Fuji
1721	Edo is believed to be the world's largest city
1772	Great Meiwa Fire – Beijing overtakes Tokyo as world's largest city
1783	Eruption of Mount Asama
1827	Captain F. W. Beechey of HMS *Blossom* claims the Ogasawara Islands for Great Britain
1830	Nathaniel Savory and several other colonists from Hawaii settle on the Ogasawara Islands
1853	Arrival in Tokyo Bay of Matthew Perry and his Black Ships; end of Japan's isolation
1854	*Odaiba* (gun emplacements) are fixed in Edo Bay
1855	Great Ansei Earthquake
1856	Hiroshige's *One Hundred Famous Views of Edo* begins publication
1858	Lord Elgin leads the first British mission to Edo
1862	*Sankin kōtai* system is suspended; massive exodus of thousands of samurai from Tokyo causes population to fall by 300,000

1868   Meiji Restoration – Battle of Ueno ends
         Shōgunal authority in the area

1869   Edo is renamed Tōkyō ('the Eastern Capital')
         and opened to foreign traders
         A fire destroys much of the area near the
         Kanda Left Gate; it is rebuilt with a shrine
         to ward off flames, and becomes known as
         Akihabara
         First rickshaws reported in Nihonbashi
         First European-style barber's shop opens in
         Ginza

1871   The new Ministry of Finance building is
         erected on the site of the Sakai Mansion;
         Masakado's grave mound is in the grounds

1872   French art critic Philippe Burty coins the
         term *Japonisme* to describe European arts
         and crafts inspired by materials newly arrived
         from Japan

1873   Opening of Ueno Park
         A fire at the Imperial Palace destroys most of
         its Tokugawa-era buildings

1877   Establishment of Tokyo University
         Edward S. Morse uncovers a shell midden in
         Ōmori
         Women are allowed back on the theatre stage
         for the first time in centuries

1881   First horse-drawn trams in Tokyo

1882   Following Japan's official annexation of the
         Ogasawara Islands, the population of ethnic
         foreigners still living there is granted Japanese
         citizenship
         Opening of Tokyo Zoo in Ueno

1883   Opening of the Rokumeikan (the 'Hall of the
         Crying Deer')
         First Chinese restaurant opens in Tokyo

1893	The Tama River valley district is returned to Tokyo, tripling the size of the prefecture
1898	Appointment of Tokyo's first mayor
1899	First coffee house opens in Tokyo
1900	The population of the Yoshiwara massively slumps after a law is passed criminalising keeping girls against their will
1903	First electric trams in Tokyo
	First European-style park, in Hibiya
	First dedicated cinema, the *Denki-kan* ('Electric Pavilion') in Akasaka
1909	A new train line connects two townships in the Yamanote area of high ground
	Iron rickshaw wheels are replaced by rubber tyres
1910	Tokugawa Yoshitoshi successfully takes off in and lands an aeroplane near what is now Yoyogi Park
	The Great Sumida River Flood destroys much of the Low City
1912	Death of Mutsuhito, the Meiji Emperor; beginning of Taishō era
1914	Completion of Tokyo Central station
1920	Dedication of the Meiji Shrine, although the grounds were still under construction
1922	Original Imperial Hotel burns down; Frank Lloyd Wright already at work on new version
1923	Great Kantō Earthquake
1925	The Yamanote train line is extended to form a loop around both upper and lower Tokyo
	Tokyo Broadcasting Station begins radio programming
	Death of Yoshihito, the Taishō Emperor, shortly before the end of the year
1926	Beginning of the Shōwa era

	First love hotel opens in Shinjuku
1927	Opening of the first subway line in Tokyo
1929	The song *Tokyo Kyōshinkyoku* ('*Tokyo March*') by Sato Chiyako is released
1931	Opening of Haneda Airport
1932	Great Tokyo City is formed by the assimilation of several nearby towns
1934	A year before his death, Hachikō the faithful hound is present at the unveiling of a statue in his honour
1936	Tokyo wins the bid to host the 1940 Olympic Games (later cancelled)
1937	Opening of Korakuen Stadium
1941	Demolition of the Rokumeikan inspires the architect Taniguchi Yoshirō to create the Meiji-Mura open-air architectural museum
1943	Tokyo City and Tokyo Prefecture are combined to make the modern metropolis
1947	US-imposed reforms to the civil lists restrict membership of the imperial family to descendants of the Taishō Emperor
1949	Amid post-war cutbacks, the government radically reduces reconstruction efforts, depriving many parts of Tokyo of modern road and rail access or properly zoned redevelopment
1951	The song *Tokyo Shoeshine Boy* by Akatsuki Teruko is released
1953	First TV broadcasts
1957	Prostitution is criminalised, although establishments soon find a number of loopholes in the law
1958	Completion of Tokyo Tower
1959	The new Tokyo Expressway is built by filling in many old city canals

1960	Tange Kenzō's futurist Plan for Tokyo proposes building out into and across the bay
1964	Shinkansen 'bullet train' opens between Tokyo and Ōsaka
	Tokyo Olympic Games
1965	Opening of the open-air architectural museum Meiji-Mura near Nagoya; despite being far from Tokyo, it preserves several important buildings from the city's past
1967	Demolition of Frank Lloyd Wright's Imperial Hotel
1968	The Ogasawara Islands, including Iwo Jima, are returned to Japanese control and included within the jurisdiction of Tokyo Municipality
1978	Opening of Narita Airport
	The names of several class-A war criminals are added to the lists of the honoured dead at the Yasukuni Shrine
1983	Opening of Tokyo Disneyland
1985	Part of Wright's Imperial Hotel is rebuilt at Meiji-Mura
1987	Agents for Yasuda Fire and Marine Insurance pay a record $39.9 million for Van Gogh's painting *Vase with Fifteen Sunflowers*
1989	Death of Hirohito, the Shōwa Emperor; beginning of the Heisei era
	Business speculator Mori Minoru starts buying parcels of land in Roppongi
1991	Opening of Tange Kenzō's Tokyo Metropolitan Government Office in Shinjuku; within the year, it becomes the site of an onscreen battle between Godzilla and King Ghidorah
1993	Opening of the picturesque Rainbow Bridge to Odaiba

1995	Aum Shinrikyō gas attack on Tokyo subway
1996	The underpopulated Odaiba business district is rezoned for commerce and entertainment
2000	Tokyo is once again believed to be the world's largest city
2003	Mori Minoru opens the Roppongi Hills development on 400 amalgamated plots of land
2012	Completion of Tokyo SkyTree
2018	Ginza Sony Park opens on the site of the corporation's old headquarters
2019	Abdication of Akihito, the Heisei Emperor
2020	Tokyo hosts the Olympics for the second time

Further Reading and References

IN COMPILING THIS BOOK, I have found the Japanese-language *Rurubu Tokyo* guide from JTB Publishing to be invaluable. The Rurubu books are magazine-format periodicals, revised annually and crammed with eye-crossingly granular accounts of hip restaurants, new tourist sites, maps and tips. The content leans heavily towards an implied reader who is a foodie and a shopper, but sites of older historical interest are not neglected. English speakers are likely to derive more immediate access to contemporary Tokyo online, from the likes of *Tokyo Time Out* (www.timeout.com/tokyo), *Metropolis* magazine (www.metropolisjapan.com) or *Tokyo Week-ender* (www.tokyoweekender.com).

Guidebooks

Taking a guidebook should no longer be a matter of fretting over space and weight, since all major versions now offer e-book editions. However, the e-book format is not the best way of dipping in and out of a large tome, and the smart reader may prefer to take a chunky Japan guide from Lonely Planet or Rough Guides in digital form alongside a sleeker, more portable Tokyo guide in paper form from the Insight Flexi Map or DK Eyewitness series.

General Accounts

The first port of call for any Tokyo historian is Edward Seidensticker's *Tokyo From Edo to Shōwa 1867–1989* (Tuttle Publishing, 2010), which not only conflates two volumes within a single cover, but also merges Seidensticker's own many years in Tokyo with that of his muse, the author and observer of Tokyo life, Nagai Kafū. Roman Adrian Cybriwsky's *Historical Dictionary of Tokyo* (Scarecrow Press, 2nd ed 2011) is too expensive for the general reader, but packed full of insightful entries, although he disagrees with Seidensticker on many matters of dating and nomenclature, including Seidensticker's own name, which he seems to think is Henry. Stephen Mansfield's *Tokyo: A Biography* (Tuttle Publishing, 2016) is a readable history of the city that can provide much local colour and insight for the visitor. The historical geographer Paul Waley has written much of interest, including *Tokyo Now & Then: An Explorer's Guide to the City* (Weatherhill, 1984) – a wonderful book, detailed enough to walk the reader through imaginary strolls like a latter-day flâneur, although at more than three decades of age, the 'now' it details is itself a historical curiosity.

Marcus Powles has self-published several books on religious tourism in the city, including *The Tokyo 33-Kannon Pilgrimage: A Guide to Ancient Edo's Sacred Path* (CreateSpace, 2014) and *Tokyo Temples: A Guide to Forty of the Best Temples of Central Tokyo* (CreateSpace, 2015). He is the first to admit that they are amateur publications and not perfect by any means – his Japanese isn't always up to explaining what he sees, but these books will certainly transform the experience of a Buddhist visitor. He's on firmer ground with *Tokyo Churches: A Guide to the Cathedrals and Churches of Central Tokyo* (CreateSpace, 2015), which is a must-buy for the visitor who wants to dive deeply into the history of Christianity in Japan and its contemporary experience in Tokyo.

For the twenty-first-century kid, or for parents out to impress their offspring with something more tailored to their interest, Gianni Simone's *Tokyo Geek's Guide* (Tuttle Publishing, 2017) reconceives a trip to the city entirely through the eyes of a manga, anime or monster movie fan, in terms of not merely attractions and shopping, but also famous locations. Geek culture moves fast, leading me to recommend it above Patrick Macias and Tomohiro Machiyama's *Cruising the Anime City: An Otaku Guide to Neo Tokyo* (Stone Bridge Press, 2004), even though Macias and Machiyama, much like Paul Waley above, chronicle a moment in time that is itself already in the past and hence of historical interest.

For a more irreverent and entertaining account of the etymology and history of certain Japanese place names, Marky Star's blog *Japan This* (www.japanthis. com) provided much helpful detail, but now only seems to be accessible through the Internet Archive Wayback Machine. For the reader interested in investigating the more general history of the entire country, you've made it this far, so why not try my *A Brief History of Japan: Samurai, Shōgun and Zen – The Extraordinary Story of the Land of the Rising Sun* (Tuttle Publishing, 2017)?

Publishers and Authors

Books about Japan rarely become bestsellers, which has led to a surprisingly strong and well-served sector of vibrant small presses serving the market. But long gone are the days when one needed to poke around a specialist bookshop to find them – online ordering and e-books can bring them all to your door at the touch of a button. Most notable is Tuttle Publishing, founded after the Second World War by a former Occupation publishing specialist, initially to bring foreign books to Japan, but soon broadening into a mission to bring Japanese works abroad. It remains a great source both for books by the Japanese themselves about their capital, and for curios like Florent Chavouet's *Tokyo on Foot* (2011), in which an artist at a loose end blunders around the city with a sketchbook. Although the influential publishing house Kōdansha International shut down in 2011, Kōdansha USA still functions as an English-language gateway to books by and about Japan and the Japanese. Stone Bridge Press, based in Berkeley, California, is a worthy purveyor of quirky books, including Rick Kennedy's *Little Adventures in Tokyo* (2012) and Arturo Silva's *Tokio Whip* (2016).

Early History

Edward S. Morse wrote several influential books about Japan, but his account of the day in 1877 when he found seashells on what was once the seashore can be found in his diary, *Japan Day By Day* (Houghton Mifflin, 1917), which also presents an entertaining and occasionally caustic account of life in Tokyo in the 1870s and 1880s. Morse thus appears in this book for two reasons, both his archaeological investigations into prehistoric Tokyo and his contemporary observations of the city in the late nineteenth century. My account of the unearthing of Tokyo artefacts also leans on Hyung Il Pai's *Heritage Management in Korea and Japan* (University of Washington Press, 2014). The best all-round account of the rise and fall of Masakado is Karl Friday's *The First Samurai* (Wiley, 2008), which goes into fine detail about his various feuds and battles, and the wild escalation of his legend after his death.

Tokugawa Edo

Constantine Vaporis' *Tour of Duty* (University of Hawai'i Press, 2008) is the best account of the phenomenon of alternate attendance, and the huge impact it had on Japan and Edo.

Although several of Ihara Saikaku's books of poetry have been published in English translation, many of them seem to have dwindled from bookstores. Ironically, the only one currently in print on Amazon is *The Great Mirror of Male Love* (Stanford University Press, 1990), which would have thoroughly scandalised many of the Japanophiles of the twentieth century for its frank portrayal of love affairs between samurai, monks and young boys.

Japanese Prints: Ukiyo-e in Edo, 1700–1900 (British Museum Press, 2010) by Ellis Tinios should be your first port of call for learning about the great artists and images of this art form. The exhibition catalogue *Hokusai: Beyond the Great Wave* (Thames & Hudson, 2017) by Timothy Clark and Roger Keyes explores many unexpected angles. Timothy Clark, again, is your man for *Kuniyoshi: From the Arthur R. Miller Collection* (Royal Academy of Arts, 2009). As for Katsushika Ōi, the artist responsible for the wonderful *Night Scene at the Yoshiwara*, few dare to speculate about the degree to which her father's artwork should really be credited to her. Katherine Govier's *The Ghost Brush* (HarperCollins, 2010; published in the UK as *The Printmaker's Daughter*) is a fictionalisation of her life, as is Hara Keiichi's animated film *Miss Hokusai* (2015).

Meiji Tokyo

The biggest and most impressive English-language account of the modernisation of Tokyo is Edward

Seidensticker's aforementioned *Tokyo From Edo to Showa 1867–1989*. Isabella Bird's comments on Tokyo derive from her letters as collected in *Unbeaten Tracks in Japan* (1880, John Murray; reprinted by Stone Bridge Press, 2006). For a more concise precis of the views of foreign visitors in the period, see Hugh Cortazzi's *Victorians in Japan: In and Around the Treaty Ports* (Athlone Press, 1987), which has supplied much of the local colour for that period in this book. My quote from Isabel Anderson in the introduction comes from her book *The Spell of Japan* (The Page Company, 1914). Quotes from Henry Faulds are from his *Nine Years in Nipon: Sketches of Japanese Life and Manners* (Gardner, 1885). Quotes from Rudyard Kipling are from Cortazzi and Webb's *Kipling's Japan: Collected Writings* (Athlone, 1988; reprinted by Bloomsbury Publishing, 2013).

John Stevenson's *Yoshitoshi's One Hundred Aspects of the Moon* (Hotei Publishing, 2014) is the best place to start with the career of this amazing artist. Although it is expensive, its high-quality printing standards do justice to the artwork, and its explanations make a crucial difference in appreciating the meaning of the images. There are e-book editions that will squirt the full set of pictures onto your iPad for a pittance, but to really appreciate Japanese art, spend a little extra so you know what you are looking at.

Shōwa Tokyo

Nothing quite evokes the absences of the war years like the Olympic Games that were scheduled but never took place. For more on this historical hiatus, see Sandra Collins, *The 1940 Tokyo Games: The Missing Olympics – Japan, the Asian Olympics and the Olympic Movement* (Routledge, 2014). For the way that Tokyo's new status as an imperial city informed its urban planning, I draw on Tristan R. Gurnow's 'Paving Power: Western Urban Planning and Imperial Space from the Streets of Meiji Tokyo to Colonial Seoul' in the *Journal of Urban History* 42(3), 2016.

Ian Jared Miller's *The Nature of the Beasts: Empire and Exhibition at the Tokyo Imperial Zoo* (University of California Press, 2013) is a wide-ranging account of this institution founded in 1883. I include it here for its heartbreaking account of the war years, when zookeepers were ordered to kill off their animals in order to preserve food and prevent the danger of an escape caused by bomb damage.

Don't take my word for it; swing by the Yasukuni Shrine gift shop and pick yourself up a copy of Tadao Takemoto and Yasuo Ohara's bilingual *The Alleged 'Nanking Massacre': Japan's Rebuttal to China's Forged Claims* (Meisei-sha, 2000), for a sense of what the place means to many of its visitors.

For more on how the Occupation colonised even the meanings of certain places in the Japanese imagination, particularly the Ginza district as revealed in *Tokyo Shoeshine Boy* and similar pop songs, see Yoshimi Shunya's essay in Sheldon Garon and Patricia Maclachlan's *The Ambivalent Consumer: Questioning Consumption in East Asia and the West* (Cornell University Press, 2006).

Heisei Tokyo

As for Tokyo's development in the post-war period, there is a wealth of books on its massive transformations. In the course of my decades of writing about Japan, I have discarded many books by visitors whose opinions are frankly worthless, but I have never been quite able to divest myself of one of the first ones that I read, George Mikes'

Land of the Rising Yen: Japan (Gambit, 1970). He tries so hard to be curmudgeonly and brusque, but you can tell that he really loves it. For an irreverent and often cutting assessment of Japanese urban development, Alex Kerr's *Dogs and Demons: The Fall of Modern Japan* (Penguin, 2001) chronicles the environmental consequences of such initiatives as the Tokyo Bay landfill project and Narita Airport. For a glimpse of a Tokyo you hope never to encounter in real life – a world of loan sharks, human trafficking, drug dealers and hostess clubs – see Jake Adelstein's well-researched *Tokyo Vice* (Constable, 2010).

Jordan Sand's *Tokyo Vernacular* (University of California Press, 2013) chronicles Japan's burgeoning sense of national heritage since the 1960s. I was alerted to the existence of Ōizumi Anime Gate by Andrew Osmond's article 'The Holy Land of Nerima' at All the Anime (www.alltheanime.com). For the story of Japan's domestic tourist transformation in the 1960s, I lean on the chapter by Yōda Tomiko in Steinberg and Zahlten's *Media Theory in Japan* (Duke University Press, 2017). My story about a famous author's youthful real-estate espionage is from Steven Poole's *Guardian* interview 'Haruki Murakami: "I'm an outcast of the Japanese literary world"', from 13 September 2014. For the argument over *omotenashi*, see Mark Schreiber's 'Has Christel Takigawa cursed Japan with her 2020 Olympics omotenashi pitch?' in *The Japan Times*, 3 February 2018. The Nomura Research Institute's seminal *Otaku Marketing* (Tōyō Keizai, 2005) has never been translated, but forms the bedrock of much of what I have to say about twenty-first-century attitudes.

The Tokyo Cheapo website (www.tokyocheapo.com) offers some quirky and illuminating advice about the city, and has a timetable of local temple festivals, fairs and jumble sales to ensure you wring the most seasonal fun out of any visit.

Eating and Drinking

If, like me, you're really serious about this subject then start with Ishige Naomichi's wonderful *The History and Culture of Japanese Food* (Routledge, 2011). Amid a number of oddly expensive books on such a cheap fast food product, George Solt's *The Untold History of Ramen* (University of California Press, 2014) is my main source for the politics of noodles. For 'Indian' curry in Japan, see Pallavi Aiyar's article 'Bose of Nakamuraya' in *The Hindu*, 6 February 2018.

To wade deep into the historical waters with Japanese beverages, try Simona Zavadckyte's *Japanese Tea: A Comprehensive Guide* (Kyoto Obubu, 2017), Jeffrey W. Alexander's *Brewed in Japan: The Evolution of the Japanese Beer Industry* (University of Hawai'i Press, 2014) and *Japanese Whisky: The Ultimate Guide to the World's Most Desirable Spirit* (Tuttle Publishing, 2018) by Brian Ashcraft et al.